Bill Dodd (1965–2024) spent his childhood in Mitchell, Queensland, and on cattle properties in the area. He left school shortly before completing year ten, after the sudden death of his stockman father. For a time he worked as a stockman near Mitchell and later on a remote cattle station in the Northern Territory.

Three days before his eighteenth birthday, Bill Dodd suffered a broken neck in a diving accident and became a quadraplegic. He spent almost six months in the spinal unit at Brisbane's Princess Alexandra Hospital, and afterwards was transferred to Westhaven Nursing Home in Roma, living there for six years. In Roma he worked as a clerical assistant in the office of the Community Youth Support Scheme.

Bill came home to Mitchell in June 1989 where he lived with his sister and family. Winner of the David Unaipon Award in 1991, *Broken Dreams* is an inspirational story about Bill's early life, told with dignity and grace.

First Nations Classics

BROKEN DREAMS

BILL DODD

UQP

First published 1992 by University of Queensland Press
PO Box 6042, St Lucia, Queensland 4067 Australia
This First Nations Classics edition published 2025

University of Queensland Press (UQP) acknowledges the Traditional Owners and their custodianship of the lands on which UQP operates. We pay our respects to their Ancestors and their descendants, who continue cultural and spiritual connections to Country. We recognise their valuable contributions to Australian and global society.

uqp.com.au
reception@uqp.com.au

Cover design by Jenna Lee
Typeset in 11.5/16 pt Bembo Std Regular by Post Pre-press Group, Brisbane
Printed in Australia by McPherson's Printing Group

Queensland Government

University of Queensland Press is supported by the Queensland Government through Arts Queensland.

Australian Government

Creative Australia

First Nations Classics are assisted by the Australian Government through Creative Australia, its principal arts investment and advisory body.

This project is supported by the Copyright Agency's Cultural Fund.

COPYRIGHTAGENCY
CULTURAL FUND

A catalogue record for this book is available from the National Library of Australia.

ISBN 978 0 7022 6919 6 (pbk)
ISBN 978 0 7022 7087 1 (epdf)
ISBN 978 0 7022 7088 8 (epub)

University of Queensland Press uses papers that are natural, renewable and recyclable products made from wood grown in well-managed forests and other controlled sources. The logging and manufacturing processes conform to the environmental regulations of the country of origin.

FSC
www.fsc.org
MIX
Paper | Supporting responsible forestry
FSC® C001695

INTRODUCTION
by Gayle Kennedy

Billy Dodd ponders
On what might have been.
He thinks of the horses he never rode
The places he has never seen
The babies he may never have
The missed opportunities in life.

I'm ashamed to say that I had never heard of Bill Dodd's amazing book until I was asked to write the introduction for this First Nations Classic edition. Bill's memoir, *Broken Dreams*, won the 1991 David Unaipon Award for an unpublished Indigenous writer, and it's a little masterpiece written with all the swagger and cheek of a young Aboriginal man from rural Australia – it's at once a tale of tragedy, gratitude and love. The reader can discover his fascinating story for themselves between its pages.

What I want to address is Bill's poem above and share something of the last eleven years of his life, which aren't written about in this memoir. Shortly after Bill died in late 2024, I had the privilege of speaking to his wife Tracy about the life they built together and the amazing things he achieved. From a troubled youth to a bestselling author. From someone destined for life on the land, sport, marriage, children, yet convinced he didn't have an artistic bone in his body, he became a prolific and successful artist who was never without a canvas of some sort in front of him, a pen or brush in his mouth. And for him the miracle of love and marriage was found with his beloved wife, Tracy – a woman who loved him as much as he loved her. He became a stepfather to her children, and even a grandfather. All the things he never thought he'd have, all those broken dreams made whole by love.

By the time Tracy came into his life, Bill had given up. Years after his tragic diving accident, he was living in a nursing home surrounded by elderly people, some with dementia, others dying, some of them constantly watching the door for visitors who never came. He had stage-four pressure sores, eleven centimetres wide. A young, vibrant man living in a body that would no longer obey him, Bill felt certain he didn't want to spend his life that way.

Tracy had escaped with her children from a bad relationship and now found herself face to face with the love of her life. Shocked and saddened by the state he was in she showered him with love and attention. He was then, and will always be, the most wonderful man she has ever met. Bill made her laugh like no-one ever had and loved her with a passion and depth she'd never experienced. They fell in love, and she took him in to live with her.

Tracy has never forgotten the look on his face when he was placed on her king-sized wooden bed covered in beautiful linen. He couldn't quite believe that this was the place he would fall asleep every night – safe and in the loving arms of his eventual wife. He told her he had never slept in a bed like that before. It remained a wonder to him. Bed had been a prison; now it was a place of joy. They were determined to make sure that their home wouldn't become a hospital and, apart from an electric bed in the living room where he'd spend his days, it remained that way.

Saturdays were Tracy's only days off and they were sacred. They would go to town, wander around, shop, eat and gossip with the townsfolk. Apparently Bill loved nothing more than a good gossip. They would watch movies in bed. They did some travelling and whatever else their hearts desired. Every year they celebrated their wedding anniversary on ANZAC Day, honouring not only their love but the long line of Black diggers who gave their lives for an often ungrateful nation.

Bill lived a rich life, not only as a husband and father but also as a successful, award-winning creative. He became a public speaker and educator on the dangers of diving headfirst into bodies of water without first checking the depth. He would go to places and speak to the young people, all ten-foot tall and bullet-proof, about how he wound up in the wheelchair. He believed it had a sobering effect on them. He believed he may have saved some lives and prevented some catastrophic accidents from happening, and I believe he was right.

Tracy faithfully tended to Bill over these years and physically took care of him right up until his final moments, where he was wrapped in her loving embrace as she promised to be there until and after his last breath. They both had a strong belief in the afterlife, and she made him promise that he would send signs that he was okay and would be waiting for her when she finally joined him. He kept his word. White cockatoo feathers would guide her path, floating by on the wind, the birds doing noisy fly-bys. Their favourite song, 'Black Boy' by Coloured Stone, would start playing in the most random places – the supermarket, a cafe, on the car radio in the middle of nowhere.

The most unusual place was one that made everyone believe that Bill was still around, although Tracy never doubted it. Bill never went on the lawn or near the garden beds, as his wheelchair was prone to getting stuck, so imagine her surprise when she noticed something glinting under the mandarin tree. It was one of Bill's drawing pens – in a place completely out of reach to Bill! This memory always makes Tracy smile. It makes me smile as well. I wish I had met him. Gotten to know him. But he lives on through this book, and his poetry and art, and the memories of those including his family and many friends and strangers whose lives he touched, and all who loved and continue to love this remarkable man.

Tracy told me that she asked him one day how a man who had suffered so much could still smile, could still love, could still be grateful every moment of his life. She said to him, 'You must have a very big heart to survive all that.' He replied, 'It's not the heart, Tracy. It's what it's connected to.' Bill Dodd was a mighty man, with a mighty spirit.

1

I am the third youngest in a family of seven. In 1965, the year I was born, my parents, Lesley and Billy Dodd (I was given the same name as my father), lived in a quiet, sleepy little country town called Mitchell, way out west. As people in the city would say: 'Mitchell? Isn't that a little one-horse place out in the sticks?' The population of Mitchell was then around 1500.

My parents were Aboriginal. My father told me: 'Always be proud of your colour, son' – and I am. I always loved to hear my people talk about the old days in Mitchell, about the yumba. The yumba was an area two miles beyond the town where all the black people used to live – only the whitefellows lived in town. Houses at the yumba had dirt floors and were lit by carbide lamps; there was no electricity. Then came the day the bulldozers moved in. The local council wanted the Murries to live in town. (The council didn't care too much what the Murries themselves thought of this idea.) Teary-eyed, the black people watched their homes being bulldozed into the ground, buried in the dust along with their treasured memories of good and bad times alike. One proud old lady remembered the fourteen children she had brought up in the yumba. She said the dirt floor of her little house 'didn't worry her'.

My brother Peter was born four years after me, and then our parents decided to leave Mitchell. My father had been offered a job as stockman on Westgrove station, twenty-three miles beyond the small town of Injune.

My uncle Edward brought his old Bedford truck to our house to lend a much needed pair of hands to load up all our belongings. I watched as my father, mother and uncle, helped as much as possible by my four older sisters – Narelle, Anne, Robyn and Michelle, whose ages went from eleven down to five – emptied our old house. After the truck was loaded and a pot of tea had been drained, it was time to say goodbye to Mitchell. Squeaks and rattles fell out of the old truck as it travelled down the road.

We seemed to travel a long time before Injune came into view. We passed through the township and finally reached Westgrove station. Then my parents and uncle unloaded the truck, putting our furniture and our other gear inside our new home before the night closed in.

We soon settled down to our new life at Westgrove. Each morning when I woke up I would find that my sisters had disappeared. I soon realised that they got up early so they'd have plenty of time to catch the school bus. It took me a while to work out where the bus stopped when it brought them back from school, but then I used to run and meet my sisters every afternoon. I can tell you that when you have four sisters older than yourself, you have to be careful to avoid an occasional clip on the ear, and know when to keep quiet. But when they were at school I used to get bored very easily. My father came to my rescue. One day he brought me a little pony and began to show me how to ride. After that, I spent all my spare time with my pony. We developed a special relationship nobody could break.

A year later, I was shocked to be told that it was time I went to school, and that I would have to leave my pony at home. I was five years old. I remember the cold, frosty winter mornings when my mother had to drag me out of bed. It was too bloody cold to go to school! It was different if I was going out mustering with my father – I would be so excited I'd be out of bed at five o'clock in the morning, no worries at all! Right from the start, in first grade, I showed signs of being a bit of a rogue. My teacher introduced me to the word 'discipline' with the help of a blackboard ruler. She had me bluffed for about two weeks. Since my four sisters were all at the same school as me, whenever I stepped out of line or played up it always got back to my mother … and she had me bluffed all the time.

I used to get myself into a bit of strife at home, too. Once I got hold of a brand-new tube of toothpaste, took a pin and put a whole heap of holes in it, so that when anyone squeezed the tube, toothpaste would ooze out all over the place. Unfortunately for me, the tube found its way into my mother's hands. When she asked who had put holes in the tube, nobody owned up. My mother said: 'Whoever owns up to the truth, I'll give them a dollar.' Then my sister Michelle said, 'I'm going to say it was me – I could use a dollar.' But as soon as she said that I piped up: 'It wasn't you, Michelle, it was me!' Michelle looked at me as if to say: 'Sucker!' I was given a good flogging. I guess Michelle was a lot smarter than I was.

We all looked forward to the school holidays, and we were never short of things to do. And for me, trouble and mischief were never far away. Riding, fishing, swimming and shooting made those holidays pass very quickly. Sometimes I used to ride my pony down to the stockyards to see my father. I would sit on the top rail, watching him handle the young horses. That was one of the things I enjoyed most.

One day, I heard Michelle let out a loud screech, and discovered that she was afraid of molly grubs. I managed to round up one of these and showed it to her. She gave another deafening squeal and took off – much to my delight. I was like a young cattle dog as I took off after her in hot pursuit. I had speed and energy to burn. In the background I could hear my mother yelling at me to leave Michelle alone. I took no notice: I never thought I would see the day my big sister would run away from me! I found that the farther I chased her, the quicker she ran. Each time she turned around and saw the molly grub in my hand, she'd put more distance between us. I never had a chance of catching her. We covered a mile or so in quick time, then Michelle ran back. As I chased her through the gate of our yard, I was met by our mum, with a big strap in her hand that sure took the smile off my face. But a flogging didn't seem to teach me anything.

A few days later, I came across my sister Robyn, who was two years older than me, sitting on the edge of the veranda. 'Billy boy, I bet you can't push me off this railing,' she said. Always ready for action, I obliged. Loud yells from an injured Robyn. Another flogging for me. I guess it goes to show that as a five-year-old, I had more guts than brains.

When I was seven, my father decided I was old enough to try riding a poddy calf. The local rodeo was coming up, and I became one of the competitors. They tied me on a little Brahmin calf and opened up the chute gate to let me into the arena. I tried my best to ride that calf, but down into the dirt I went. I picked myself up out of the dust with a bloody nose, a few tears and a pretty damn sore ego. All this for a lousy two dollars – but nevertheless that reward took away a lot of the pain.

All my love was for horses. Out riding, if I fell off I always got back on. One afternoon I returned from school to find a pretty little Palomino pony tied up in the yard at home. My father told me he had named her 'Tina'. Apparently as a yearling, Tina had been branded an outlaw, considered unmanageable. But Dad had taken a liking to the pony and paid her former owner ten dollars for her. He then broke in Tina himself, and soon found that all she needed was a little bit of love and plenty of patience, which he gave her. He was rewarded: the fiery little horse was soon quietened as Dad gained her full trust. Now, Tina had become so quiet that Dad had brought her home for us kids to ride.

I took a real liking to Tina. Each day after school I used to ride the pony across the creek, so that she could have a clear drink of water from the trough on the other side. When Tina and I came to the creek we used to walk down one side, and as soon as we got to the bottom I would gallop her up the other side. This was a lot of fun for anyone who could ride really well. My sisters Michelle and Anne, however, found out that it wasn't much fun if you couldn't ride properly. Michelle, in fact, couldn't ride at all, so Anne said: 'Jump up here behind me, Michelle – I'll look after you.' As Tina set off slowly down the road the girls were progressing well, but as they approached the river, trouble was not very far away. Tina walked quietly down the near side of the creek and then, just as I'd taught her, she took off flat, galloping straight up the opposite bank.

The pony made it up the bank okay, but my two sisters were left floundering in the water, while Tina stood waiting for them to mount her again and ride home. Quite soon I saw the two girls coming back along the road, leading the pony. As they drew closer I saw that their backsides were riddled with burrs. My sisters were cursing loudly and blaming me for what had happened – they were out for my blood.

It was in grade three that I began to get the occasional blood nose or busted lip. I never knew how to fight back.

But one day, after I'd received yet another bleeding nose, I knew it was time I did so. My father told me: 'If you don't learn to fight, those other blokes will walk all over you. Even if you don't win every time, make sure you let them know you were there.' He gave me some useful pointers, and next morning, scared shitless though I was, I was keen to get to school and try out his advice. I soon found the kid who'd given me a bleeding nose the day before. I just wanted to flatten *his* nose. I lined this kid up from a long way back and came at him swinging punches. I think it was fear that made me clean miss with my first punch. But my second came into solid contact with the kid's nose. He took off, and I found that he left me alone after that. My father had been right.

I used to get into a few fights whenever someone called me a 'black bastard'. School kids can be pretty nasty and they know how to hit below the belt with remarks like that. One day in class, a bloke called me a 'nigger'. Because we were in the classroom, he didn't think I'd be game to do anything about it. But I got up off my chair and punched this bloke right under the teacher's gaze. My punishment was two hits of the cane and having to spend the rest of the day chipping burrs in the school yard. It was worth it. I was proud to be a Murri.

During the school holidays I continued to spend a lot of time at the cattle yards on the property. I enjoyed watching the ringers draft the cattle they had mustered. Sometimes, my father would take me with him on the shorter mustering trips. Dad used to ride one of the young horses he'd recently broken in. Some of them were really fresh and would start to buck as soon as they were mounted. My father was so cool. He would come into the yard, roll a smoke, have a bit of a yarn, then climb into the saddle. After he had given the horse a bit of a workout in the yard, it was time to go mustering.

My Uncle Edward gave me a black-and-white sheep dog. I named him 'Snip', and we had plenty of fun together. I was old enough now to do my share of the chores about the place. I had to feed and water the chickens, brush and feed Tina, water the dogs, gather firewood and cut the logs. My father trusted me with all these jobs – until one day he found out how I'd been spending part of my time. He decided to go down to the wood heap and do some chopping. Grabbing a block of wood, he found a nice little pile of contraband hidden there: a tin of Log Cabin tobacco, two packets of Benson and Hedges cigarettes, one packet of Craven A, and a couple of boxes of matches. My punishment was a good old-fashioned kick up the arse.

In 1973 my youngest sister, Donna, arrived, the only one of our family to be born in Injune. All the rest of us were born in Mitchell. Four months later, our parents decided to leave Westgrove and go back to live in Mitchell – my father had been offered a new job, working on Mount Owen station. We had lived at Westgrove for four years, and during that time I had adapted to the stillness and quietness of the bush. My love for the bush and its inhabitants had grown enormously. We had tamed a few little kangaroo rats and one or two wild cats. I was really sorry to leave Westgrove. When we moved back to Mitchell, my father would be working in the bush while we would be living in town. That meant no more freedom, no more peace, and, worst of all, no more horse or dog. Tina, the little Palomino pony and my dog Snip would be out in the bush with my dad.

Another day of moving arrived. Once again, Uncle Edward brought his old Bedford truck, this time to take us back to Mitchell. When we started to move our gear, two of the wild cats I had caught and tamed disappeared – maybe they could sense that we were going to live in town, and decided they wanted to remain in the bush, together with the other kids and the animals.

As I sprawled in the back of the old truck later that day, I was really sorry to see the last of Westgrove station. I waved goodbye to the bush. Five minutes later, the place that had been my home for the past four years disappeared around a bend in the road.

2

Back in Mitchell, we settled into a house with one of our aunties, and a week later my father returned to the bush, to work on Mount Owen station. We stayed with our auntie for a few months before we found a place of our own in Mitchell.

My father used to stay out in the bush for months at a time, coming back to town for a few days. Then back he would go to his beloved bush and the horses he loved so dearly. I have never known a man who loved horses as much as Dad.

I soon found that town life was very different to the peace and freedom of the bush. At Westgrove I'd had plenty of room to kick a football, but in town I was told to be careful and give some consideration to our next-door neighbour. I was guilty more times than once of kicking my football onto our neighbour's roof. It would land on the roof with a loud bang and I used to have about ten seconds to put my fingers in my ears – you could be sure as hell that the old girl, my Mum, would crack up.

I was now in grade four at Mitchell State School. At first some of the other kids would pick a fight with me, but they soon left me alone when I showed them I wasn't scared of anyone and was ready to fight back – the lesson I'd learned from my father back in grade three.

A few months after our return to Mitchell, my father arrived in town with a little brown-and-white pony. Dad and I named this pony 'Billyjack'. After riding the pony for most of the day, I asked my father if I could go for one more ride on him.

'Take those two pieces of wood I've cut and put them inside, then you can go for another ride,' my father said.

Thinking that he'd left the scene – I'd seen him walk off behind the bathroom – I muttered to myself, 'Do it yourself, ya old bastard'. I nearly died as I received a kick up the arse (and they say Mal Meninga has a good right foot). 'Did I hear you say something, son?' my father asked. I was a bit shell-shocked as I replied: 'Would you like me to pick up the rubbish in the yard as well – it's no trouble.' For me, that was a lesson learned the hard way.

My dad toed me up the arse a few more times, but even today I have never forgotten that I was in the wrong always. Usually when any of us kids stepped out of line it was the old girl who pulled us back, using a strap. Mum was tough – but fair. I had to do my homework each night under her supervision.

When I reached grade six at school, I ran into one teacher I reckoned was a bit of a bastard, and probably he thought the same about me. He lived by the law of the blackboard ruler and I received my fair share of hits, together with the rest of the class. In grade seven, however, I met one of the nicest teachers going: Mrs Wichlacz. She was so caring, and treated everyone the same. Yet she wasn't soft: she faced facts and she took a person for what they were. You couldn't help but like this lady. She made you really want to try hard to pass exams. I first met Mrs Wichlacz over the holidays, when I was on my way to the bush with my father. We stopped at Polana, the halfway point between Mitchell and Mount Owen – Mrs Wichlacz lived there with her husband. She was the only teacher I have ever trusted.

As a fresh-faced twelve-year-old I met a few of the characters working out in the bush. I loved to listen to their stories, and when they spoke of cowboys, stockmen and ringers, straight away the one person who came into my mind was my father, Billy Dodd.

My father, Billy Dodd, was very proud to be Aboriginal. He was dark-skinned, a very shy, quiet man. He was not very tall, not very broad – there was really not much to this man at all when you looked at him. But he was a very understanding man and very special to everyone in his family. He also had some old-fashioned ideas – he believed that necklaces, earrings and bangles were strictly for girls, that Slim Dusty was number one, and that the only type of haircut for a man was short back and sides. My brother Peter and I used to disappear at the mention of a haircut, but the truth was, my bloody ears were too big.

My father had a special way with horses, whether he was handling them from the ground or up in the saddle. Over the years he had carved his name as a horseman and a breaker. Men like Lyle Kearns, who worked alongside my father, tell me he was one of the best. They say he could tame a horse when the devil stirred inside it. He was afraid of nothing and would ride anything with four legs. He was a stockman made and born. I spent all the time I could with my father, watching him break in the young horses. I soon got to appreciate his riding ability, his coolness, and his patience. My father won my respect and admiration.

One day, Dad received a setback when he was breaking in a young horse. It lashed out with a back leg and caught him on the knee. He went away to Brisbane to have an operation, and after that he had a permanent limp. But he returned to the bush, to the only job he'd ever known. He was a lot slower at getting up on the young horses after that, but he'd grown up tough and refused to give in. I was twelve at this time, and had to wait for the school holidays to come round before I could go back to join my father in the bush. Like him, I was growing up around horses and enjoyed their company more than that of most of the people I met. During the next holidays, I noticed that my father was a lot slower – there were times when I found my hands over my face and my heart in my mouth, but somehow he managed to go on working with the horses. Around this time, he left Mount Owen to go contract mustering on Possession Creek station.

At the end of those holidays I returned to town and went back to school – it was always good to see my mates again, Alan Martin, David Nixon, Michael Cambarngo and Adrian Finlay. They were my closest friends. I used to go jogging each afternoon after school finished. I recall very well the day I returned home from one of my jogs, when another of my mates, Michael Kearns, whistled out to me. When I ran over to him, he told me that my father had died. I couldn't believe it. I wouldn't believe it. I just wanted to punch my mate and tell him it wasn't true.

Unfortunately, the moment I arrived home I knew it was true. My mother told me that Dad had stepped off his horse to throw a mickey – a young bull. After he'd thrown the mickey his horse trotted away from him, and when my father chased after the horse, he suffered a heart attack. This devastating piece of news was the biggest kick in the arse I ever received.

As a kid, I had been told that only sooks cry. I ran downstairs, out of the house, and sat on a log. I stared into space, picturing my father in my mind, remembering the shy man known to me as Billy Dodd, or simply 'Dad'. My horse, Billyjack, was in the yard where I was sitting. I was okay until Billyjack walked over to me and started chewing on my hair. I threw my arms around my horse's neck, fighting back in the tears which I could no longer hold. I cried, feeling alone and unwanted. I never felt so sad in my life as I did that day. I had never thought my father might die; he was only forty-five and he seemed so fit and healthy. Unknown to me, however, he was a sick man. After that day, our family's strong spirit was broken and replaced by grief.

My mother told me stories about my father when he was a boy. At school he was nicknamed 'The Inspector', she said, because he used to turn up at school about as often as the school inspectors did. My father was a bugger of a boy when it came to school attendance.

He used to ride to school and hide his horse in the bush. He'd go into the classroom until he heard the bell for little lunch. Then he'd jump the fence, get on his horse and swim in the saddle across the Maranoa river. In those days, the police sergeant, who had the task of getting my father and any other truants to stay at school, rode a pushbike around the town. But by the time my father had swum his horse across the river, the poor old sergeant would still be pedalling flat out on his pushbike, just coming over the bridge. When my dad reached the other side of the river he would turn around and give the police sergeant the forks.

But like the saying goes, 'every dog has his day' – and the poor old sergeant had his day, all right. This day, my father was doing his usual stunt. When the little lunch bell rang, he ran down and got on his horse. As he was cantering away from the sergeant, the horse fell over and threw him hard on the ground.

It fairly knocked the stuffing out of him. My father lay on the ground for a while, winded. He couldn't get up in time to escape the clutches of the sergeant. The sergeant, pedalling hell for leather, was relieved when he saw the horse fall. He went over and picked my father up, then gave him a good talking to, a kick up the arse, and took him back to school.

Dad and his brother, Johnny, were at school together. What a pair of outlaws! One day they decided to wag school. Johnny hid their schoolbags under the floorboards of the house, while my father stood watch. 'There, Bill, no one will find those bags,' he said ... then he looked around and to his great surprise he saw a size ten, brand-new shiny black boot: it belonged to the police sergeant. My father had seen the sergeant coming and bolted, leaving Johnny to talk his way out and enable the sergeant to break in one shiny black boot with yet another kick in the arse.

My father had left school after completing grade four. Then he started working with his father.

As time progressed, I found that many things began to fall apart following my father's death. I was allowed a lot more freedom; floggings and the strong discipline of home life ended. I don't think my mother cared any more. I now realise that a lot of young people take their parents for granted – they don't appreciate them until they haven't got them any more, and then it's too late.

After my father's death I didn't care about anything at all except my horse Billyjack. My horse was the only one who understood me, no matter what sort of a mood I was in. My horse was a true and faithful mate.

At the time Dad died I was still only twelve. When I went back to school I found I had lost all my interest in it, and by the time I turned thirteen I positively hated going to school. I spent most of my time outside the classroom or down at the office.

When I got to grade nine, I had a lot of fun wagging school to go horseriding. I used to go to school mostly on Wednesdays, as that was the day we played sport, mostly rugby league. Out of all the teachers in high school I liked only one, a bloke named Jon Ikin. He took us for football and cricket training and you could have a bit of a joke with him. He was a good bloke. I made it to grade ten, but never completed the year.

Before I left school I won the high school cross-country race and was senior boy champion in athletics. I received two medals from the principal, Mr Burrows, who liked me about as much as I liked him – very little. It must have been hard for Mr Burrows to present me with two medals. For a change he had to be nice to me. This was the first time I'd put out my hand to him for something other than the cane. It was after this double feat that I decided to leave school.

3

After I left school I found myself a job looking after and tailing a mob of cattle and a few thousand head of sheep. Out in the bush, I used to lie awake each night thinking about my father. One night I set myself a goal in life: to become a cowboy, stockman or a ringer just like my father. If I turned out half the man my father had been then I would be happy.

I worked at this job for a few months and enjoyed it, even though I was paid only ten dollars a day. I understood that my boss was suffering from the drought and was forced to move some of his stock off the property, putting the cattle and sheep on agistment to try to save his livelihood. While I worked here I stayed in an old tin shed. I had to boil water to bathe, and the toilet was a big box tree. It was a rough camp, but I didn't mind. For me this was a good job. I gained a ton of experience, looking after horses, cattle and sheep. I really understood horses and felt good working with them. My goal in life was slowly coming together.

Some four months later I left this job and came back

to town. One night I ran into Michael Cambarngo and Alan Martin, a pair of outlaws at the best of times, but two top blokes. Later on, we decided to get on the grog to ease the boredom. Like a dickhead I took a liking to Port 99 and beer, with the result that around midnight, I found myself in more strife than I could handle. At the age of sixteen I had my first taste of jail. I was locked up in the watch house in Mitchell, my home town. I can tell you that was one of the coldest nights of my life. The policeman who locked me up threw me a blanket, the roughest, prickliest one I'd ever felt. Even so, I bloody near froze. The temperature was minus one degree Celsius on the thermometer. To make things worse, I was woken at two o'clock in the morning to be questioned. The sergeant informed me that I had called him a 'fat bastard'. I was giving cheek and when he came over towards me I apparently said, 'Catch me if you can, you fucking copper,' and he did. I was too drunk to run away – he tackled me on the cement and put me in the police car. I couldn't remember saying or doing these things. To tell the truth, I think I'd hurt the sarge's feelings a bit – he was in a really bad mood when he questioned me. He told me a few more things that I'd done, and then everything started coming back to me. Boy, was I in the shit! I'd told the police I was eighteen, when in fact I was still only sixteen. Then the sergeant decided to give my mother a ring. 'Mrs Dodd, we have your son Bill here at the watch house,' he told her. 'It will be eighty dollars to bail him out.'

'Leave him there until the morning,' my mother replied.

The police kept on questioning me, then decided to call my mother again. The sarge lowered my bail to forty dollars. But once again the old girl proved stubborn. 'I'll bail him out in the morning,' she said. When the sarge found out I was broke, he lowered my bail right down to two lousy bucks, and finally offered to pay my way out of jail himself. He was pretty disgusted when I told him to keep his money and lock me up again – to tell the truth, I couldn't face the long cold walk back home. The sarge just toed me up the arse and sent me on my way.

In the next few weeks, I rode a young horse around town to quieten it down for its owner and get it used to traffic. For this simple job I was given another horse for myself, a little brown gelding I named 'Four X'.

A month or so passed without incident. Until twelve o'clock one night, when Bodge Burns, Adrian Finlay and myself were sitting outside the cafe, drinking stubbies. I got up to go around to the back of the cafe to have a leak. When I came back, I was just in time to see the two of them getting into a white car.

'Wait for me, you pair of bastards!' I sang out to my mates. And that was when I heard a familiar voice call out: 'Grab that other bugger, too.' Too late I realised that I should have stayed at the back of the cafe – and the next moment I came face to face with the police sergeant. I decided to take off, and was lucky that I could run a bit.

I streaked off down a dark alley. Bodge and Adrian were driven home in the police car.

A few weeks later, my horse Four X saved me from being locked up. I was riding my horse home from the pub, blind drunk, when I heard the police car come up behind me and stop. A policeman grabbed me off my horse and put me in the car. Since I had only one block to go before I got home, the other policeman said he would lead the horse home. But Four X was tired and didn't lead well at the best of times. I used Four X as a kids' pony, so he was also a bit spoilt. Now he found a sweet patch of grass, and that was where he decided to stay. He was bailing up the long arm of the law, refusing to move. The second policeman let me out of the car and legged me back on my horse, and Four X and I were escorted home together.

At sixteen, I guess you could say I was very immature. I thought everything I did was always right, and could see no wrong in my wild ways. I enjoyed a drink and a fight. I refused to listen to anyone or take a single piece of advice. I had another trip to jail and seemed to be staring at a spell in Boggo Road when I got older. One of the Mitchell policemen, Mort Faddy, told me that if I didn't shout him a beer when I turned eighteen, in return for all the trouble I'd caused him already, he'd lock me up for sure. We shook hands on it – he wasn't a bad bloke.

This was the time when my Uncle John, usually known as JD, came into my life. I took a liking to him the first time I saw him, and willingly agreed to go out into the bush to give him a hand with some young horses. I was glad to have the chance to get out of town for a while, for I'd certainly got myself into a fair bit of strife in a very short time.

So my uncle and I split the scene for a while. He took me to a place called the Womals, a few hours by car from Mitchell. We collected a mob of unbroken horses from some stations close to the Womals, and transported them to our camp. In the following weeks I was in for a shock or two. I came out to the Womals as a cocky sixteen-year-old, thinking I would be able to ride most of the horses for sure. A week later I was walking around wondering if I could ride any horse at all. Some of those horses at the Womals taught me a few lessons I've never forgotten. JD had educated a few other cocky kids. He knew I wasn't a bad kid if I was treated right, so he'd decided to take me under his wing as his offsider. I sure had a lot to learn, but he was willing to give me a chance.

The first day we ran the mob of unbroken horses into the yard we'd rigged up and threw a rope over the head of a big chestnut gelding. After two days, the big gelding had been handled and quietened down enough to put my saddle on its back. Later that afternoon, the chestnut was ready for his first ride. I felt a bit uneasy as I grabbed a handful of mane and pulled myself into the saddle. I felt my foot land in the opposite stirrup iron and knew I was on. All of a sudden I felt the gelding go down into a low crouch, and it was at that moment that I knew all my Christmases had come at once. The chestnut horse leapt high into the air and took off at a horrifying pace. The old bush saying, 'He's dropped his head' was all I could think about as the horse began to buck. Just the way I'd seen it at the rodeos, I threw one hand high in the air – and guess what, I followed it and landed on my arse on the ground. I picked myself up out of the dirt and dust, wondering where the hell I'd gone wrong. After uttering a few threats and giving a shake of the head, I climbed back on and gave that chestnut a good workout, and stepped off him again without any further trouble. I'd learned my first lesson the hard way. After I'd taken my saddle and bridle off the horse and let him go with the others, my uncle and I decided to call it a day. We'd be back next morning to give the chestnut his second ride. My Uncle John was grinning like a shot fox when he saw me thrown off the chestnut – the old bugger, he thought it was a great joke.

That night I was restless, haunted by the day's events. I had ridden one horse and been thrown. How many more times would that happen?

Next morning I felt a bit winky as I checked my gear. I caught the chestnut horse and threw my saddle on his back once more. He just crow-hopped around the yard, no problem. A few more rides and that big chestnut never gave any more trouble: he was well on the way to being broken in. A month later he was quiet enough to be taken home. His owner arrived with a horse float. In a way I was sorry to see the last of him.

The next horse I had to work down was a little grey Welsh mountain pony, a bit taller than a Shetland.

I took one look at that grey pony and thought: this will be a piece of cake. A couple of rides, I told myself, and anyone should be able to ride him. I was fairly keen to get the Welsh pony going so that I'd be able to take some of the other horses for a ride. I put my saddle on loose to begin with and tightened the girth gradually, as most young horses are very touchy when you do this. I grabbed the reins up short and climbed into the saddle. As soon as I stepped on I knew the grey pony was going to buck. I could tell just by the way he was walking around the yard. He kept putting his head down. Like a sucker, I hit him on the shoulder with my reins. What happened next occurred in a split second. Once again I picked myself up out of the dust. I noticed that my saddle had worked its way too far forward; as a result I was pivoted straight over the horse's ears into the dirt.

I was thrown twice more off the little grey Welsh mountain pony, but eventually worked him down with a lot of time and effort. That Welsh pony left me with the feeling that he could have thrown me anyhow, anywhere, anytime.

Everything was going well for me – I enjoyed working with the horses and being in the bush. But our food supply was getting low, and it was time to go to town to get more supplies.

After being in town for a day I decided to ride downtown to get a dozen stubbies. On my way home I met a girl my own age and we began chatting. We were both under-age drinkers, and she said: 'Go down under the bridge and I'll come down and have a beer with you.' So she jumped up behind me and we headed down under the bridge on my horse. If I'd had a car everything would probably have worked out all right, but as I rode my horse down the girl's brother must have seen us and gone home to tell their mother. We drank the stubbies and I went for a ride.

Later that afternoon I was sitting on Four X talking to my mates Adrian Finlay and Wally Fuller. All of a sudden I heard a car pull up behind me and heard a woman's voice: 'You – Bill Dodd! I want to see you over at my place in an hour's time or I'll report you to the police.' She was the girl's mother.

So an hour later, Adrian and I rode over to the girl's home to see what her mother wanted. Adrian filled me with confidence. 'Don't worry, I'll keep an eye on the windows just in case she pulls out a gun.' After that comment I was ready to bolt at the drop of a hat. If the girl's mum shot off a gun the way she shot off her mouth, then Adrian and I were two dead coons.

Out through the front door of the house came the woman, her mouth firing on all cylinders. (She first softened me up by telling me she could knock me out with a single punch.) She was giving me heaps. While I had put up with her ranting and raving, Adrian was killing himself with laughter. He thought it was a great joke. He made me smile every now and then, which made the girl's mother snap: 'If you think this is all a joke then you can come down to the police station right now.' I can tell you I was happy to get away from her alive.

After that weekend, my uncle, JD, turned up at five o'clock on Monday morning to take me back into the bush. I was really pleased to get away, though at times I used to wonder what I was doing there, in the stillness and quietness. Sometimes I felt like a Queen Street cowboy, one of those blokes who comes out to the country from the city and gets all done up in cowboy gear when he hasn't even seen a horse, let alone ridden one.

At the Womals it was back to work. I went down to the horse yard and caught the Welsh mountain pony. After its few days off the little pony went really well, so I took off my saddle and decided to ride bareback. Everything went well until I rode past an old tin shed. Just as my pony and I walked around the corner of the shed, a big black chicken ran out from the dark shadows inside, and straight under the pony's belly. The pony's reaction was to take off and jump high in the air. I thought he was never going to come back to earth, and when he did – I left him. (Not by my own choice.) I picked myself up off the ground really quickly; I didn't want my uncle to see that I'd been thrown yet again. But the first thing I heard was loud laughter, and I caught sight of a number of people looking at me from the shed windows. I picked up my sore ego and jumped back on the pony. I don't know which of us had got the bigger fright – me, the pony or the chicken. By now, the workers in the shed had positioned themselves on the top rail of the fence, expecting more trouble to enjoy. They looked like a flock of prize parrots perched there. The little grey pony and I disappointed them. We continued on our way just as though nothing had happened. My uncle never said a word, just smiled to himself.

Next day, he lined us both up for a few days' work on another property. Our job was to muster about 1500 head of sheep for shearing. In the morning, much to my disgust, I was woken at five o'clock. I still felt half asleep as I went down to the horse yards and caught a young bay mare that I had never had anything to do with before. I plonked on my saddle and tightened up the girth, then put one foot in the stirrup iron and climbed aboard. Everything seemed to be going well, but as I got down the road a bit I was in for a shock. The mare dropped her head and started to buck. I did not get very far down the road, and I was fully awake as I came into solid contact with the hard ground. I was none too pleased when the station boss came over on his motorbike and said: 'Gee, son, you've got a graceful way of falling off!' After that I stayed awake on the big bay, but at the end of the day I was nearly caught off guard again. Once more the bay mare dropped her head and started to buck. I was all arms and legs, but managed to stay in the saddle for a change. I took one look at the ground and it was too damn hard to fall off this time.

After the shearing we returned to the Womals. All together we had twenty-four horses there, most of them young ones. Although I sure had my fair share of busters, quite often I managed to stay in the saddle when a horse started to buck. But that doesn't make such a good story! After my uncle and I had done all we could with the horses we returned them to their owners. Then it was time to move on.

We went back to town and got a job working racehorses. I used to have to get out of bed at five-thirty each morning, which nearly killed a lazy bugger like me, so that we could make an early start on the horses. In winter it was so cold that I used to have tears trickling down the side of my face and couldn't feel my fingers as I exercised each horse. You had to be crazy to work those racehorses in winter. As the weather warmed up things became easier.

One morning I was hung over with too much grog from the night before. The last place I wanted to be was out there, exercising those racehorses. However, I got to work, and finally there was only one horse left to ride. I caught that last horse and set off. Coming around the corner of the track, the horse shied at a pigeon sitting there. I wasn't sure if the horse had seen the fence to the left of me, so I loosened my grip on the reins. At the same moment the horse hit the fence and stopped dead. I was gently thrown over the fence and landed on the broad of my back.

All the times I was thrown from horses I was never hurt too bad. I had horses fall over with me, I got thrown hard onto the ground, I even had horses rear over backwards. But I always managed to walk away unhurt.

I still lacked discipline. One night my mates Michael Cambarngo, Chong, Adrian Finlay and a few others decided to get on the grog. Since some of us were under-age and not able to drink at the pub, we decided to get a carton of stubbies and drive around in Ernie's taxi. Ernie charged us twenty cents to beep the horn, twenty cents to do a fishhook, fifty cents to spin the wheels and a dollar to do a handbrake. By the end of the night we had fitted seventeen blokes in the taxi, with another one hanging off the roof rack.

My uncle and I spent a few months working the racehorses, and then I gave this job away, and we broke our partnership. But I shall never forget how Johnny Dodd taught me such a hell of a lot in such a short time.

4

There wasn't much work around Mitchell, so a bloke called Greg Pearce and I decided to head up to the Northern Territory. I felt, too, that I needed to get out of Mitchell for a while. Greg and I already had a job lined up in the Territory, at a station called Auvergne, two hundred kilometres out of Katherine.

We headed off by coach, waving to our mates as we pulled out of the bus depot. The trip to Mt Isa seemed to pass reasonably quickly, but when we got there we were told that the road was too wet for the bus to continue the journey. Passengers travelling to the Northern Territory would have to stay a few days in Mt Isa. Greg and I were in luck. I don't think we had a dollar between us, but one of the other passengers on the bus told us we could stay at his place. During the next few days we became accustomed to the scene at Mt Isa, but we were eager to get to our destination.

On the bus once more, we seemed to travel for hours before the driver at last pulled up for lunch at a little outback pub. As Greg and I stepped off the bus, we were only too well aware of the stares of the local drinkers. To make things worse, there were thousands of grasshoppers. You had to be pretty watchful, especially if you were munching on a steak sandwich. If you felt something that was a bit crunchy and tasted bloody awful, then it paid not to swallow it. While we were there, one of the blokes grabbed a grasshopper and snuck up behind this girl. He put the grasshoper down the back of her t-shirt. The girl let out a cooee and, boy, did she cut some capers – much to the delight of her tormentor and the onlookers drinking in the pub. These were wild boys, the type that make the bush proud. 'If this is the Territory, take me home!' I told Greg.

Then we were back on the road. Greg and I spent a day and a night on the bus before we arrived at a place called Threeways, the junction where all the buses met and fuelled up before taking off in three different directions. Greg and I wanted to get on the bus for Katherine, and we caught what we hoped was the right one. Travelling along the highway, we weren't sure whether we were on the right bus or not. Greg was only fifteen, I was just a year older, and we were both really shy and didn't feel game enough to go on up and ask the driver if we were in fact on the way to Katherine. We sat there like two stuffed dummies – until I realised that if we were on the wrong bus, it was quite serious. Forgetting my shyness, I leapt out of my seat and went up to the driver. I was one happy bloke when he named Katherine as his destination.

We finally arrived at Katherine about ten o'clock next morning, and from the bus stop we were driven out to the airstrip, where we sat on our swags expecting someone to come along in a car or truck to take us the last two hundred kilometres of our journey. Suddenly a young, skinny fellow approached us and asked our names. We told him. 'You're the two boys I have to take out to Auvergne,' he said. 'Come over and throw your gear into that little blue plane over there.'

Straight away I wanted to bail out. Flying was not for me! I was scared of heights – at home in Mitchell, even the house roof was too high for me. I felt safe firmly rooted to the ground. I had always wanted to go to New Zealand, but wouldn't travel by ship in case it sank in the sea, and I wouldn't travel by plane in case it fell out of the sky. And now Greg and I were expected to fly to Auvergne.

All Greg could say was, 'I want the front seat!' He could have the whole bloody plane for all I cared. Somehow, getting up all my courage and with my poor old legs feeling like jelly, I managed to climb in the back. I still don't really know how the pilot and Greg between them conned me on board, and I can't recall very much about the flight – but I was sure glad to step out and feel the ground beneath my feet once more when we arrived! I couldn't get away from that little blue plane quick enough. 'That Billy's a quiet boy,' said the pilot.

Auvergne was a big place, bigger than any station I'd known before. You could go ninety kilometres in one direction and still not reach the boundary. We soon settled in and began work with the horses. But that first week I nearly blew it. One morning, Greg and I went down to the horse yards on our own and started riding some of the young horses without supervision. As a result I got a smack on the jaw from the head stockman. Luckily for me, he couldn't hit real hard. I told him to stick his job. Feeling that I had made better starts in a new place, I went to get my gear, ready to leave – then the boss appeared and told me I still had my job. But I was removed from being with the horses to working in the house yard. I had to mow, rake the lawn and pick up fallen leaves. Talk about ruining a cowboy's reputation!

Then we were told we'd be working on a muster using helicopters. Before it started we had a free weekend and one of the ringers, a young bloke called Geoff Miller, took Greg and me to swim in the river. I dived in and swam about eighty metres to the other side, to sunbake on some rocks. As I lay in the sun I sang out to Geoff: 'Hey, let's go fishing!'

'No fish here, mate – the crocs eat them all out,' Geoff replied.

Crocs! Shit, I'd forgotten all about crocs being in the Territory. In Mitchell, the nearest thing to a crocodile would be a goanna. Lying on those rocks, I wasn't sure if I should risk swimming back to the other side of the river. Geoff had put the fear of God into me. I guess a real hero like me shouldn't mention my two kilometre jog upstream to the safety of shallow water. The crocs would have to wait a while if they planned to eat this Murri.

Two days later the muster was under way, with the cattle being rounded up by helicopter. The Auvergne cattle sighted men only twice a year. They were wild and toey. When a muster was completed, the blokes would have to pull down the portable yards they set up. These were made out of steel panels – they needed to be extra strong because some of those cattle were really wild, charging at men and the panels alike.

We'd give each mob some time to cool off after being rounded up before drafting began. Drafting took one or two days, depending on how many the helicopter had managed to muster. We branded the calves and put them back with their mothers. Bulls, bullocks and mad cattle were sent to the meatworks. All weaners were tailed out – they soon settled down to feed instead of running away.

At sixteen, I had no experience with such wild cattle. You learn from your mistakes. One day, as we were drafting a mob, I was working the dividing gate for the cattle being sent to the meatworks. Leaning on the gate, I was laughing at this mad bullock that kept charging my mate. My back was turned towards the cattle in the yard. All of a sudden this other big bullock charged at me. I don't know what made me turn round, but I did – and just caught a glimpse of him coming straight towards me. I sidestepped, just in time and the bullock crashed into the gate right where I'd been standing. I might have needed a new pair of pants after that. I stood there, shaking. Two hours later I was still shaking.

After about three weeks, Greg and another stockman quit the job. We were being paid $100 a week minus tax. We started work at seven each morning and finished when the job was done, sometimes early, sometimes late. After each muster we had a few days off, and every Friday night there was a barbecue at the station, which was good. I liked the job – it brought me new experiences. To tell the truth, it was a job that turned boys into men.

While I was at Auvergne I rode a grey horse that was a bit of an outlaw; whenever I got on his back he would buck high and hard. But rough as that grey horse was, I never had any trouble staying in the saddle. At sixteen, I proved that I could ride a horse. I had matured over the past months, and the time I spent with my uncle had finally paid off.

I stuck this job out for a few more months. I'm not real sure why I left it in the end. But I had a girlfriend back in Mitchell, and at times I felt a bit homesick. Auvergne was in the middle of nowhere … no grog, no women. So one weekend, when we were going to Katherine for the rodeo, I packed up my gear and put it in the car. I stayed in a motel at Katherine, and two days later caught the bus and came back to Queensland. I really liked the Northern Territory, though, and afterwards I was sorry I'd left. I always swore I would return there when I was a bit older, a bit tougher and a bit wiser.

5

At the end of the long journey home, I was more than happy when the bus stopped at Mitchell. I stepped off it and walked home. The first thing I did was to get my faithful horse, Four X. I jogged six kilometres out to the place where he was being kept, caught him and rode him back into town.

That Sunday was the last round of the football. I got a game that weekend, playing second row for the under-eighteen Mitchell Magpies. I played in the following six games, and we found ourselves in the grand final. I had never thought about playing in a grand final, let alone winning it. But win it we did!

Next day, the boys got on the grog to celebrate the win. We were doing a pub crawl, and Four X provided transport for Michael Cambarngo and myself to each pub we visited. To begin with we tied up Four X outside, but when we arrived at the Mitchell Hotel, Michael and I decided that Four X was doing such a top job he should join us inside. So Michael opened the pub doors. I rode over to the bar and ordered 'Two beers, please, one for me and one for my horse.' The barman kicked us out. 'There was only one reason why we got kicked out of that pub,' I told Michael. 'The bloody horse is under-age.'

A few weeks later, I found a job mustering on a place called Mount Elliott. I enjoyed working there. Two of my mates, Adrian Finlay and Angus Mitchell, were also at Mt Elliott. Adrian and I shared a room. One night, when I had just dozed off, I was suddenly woken by Adrian. He was sitting up in bed pointing at the roof and saying: 'Dingoes, dingoes – quick, get me the gun!' Then he shook his head and said: 'Too late, you mob of useless bastards, they're gone.' When I looked closely at Adrian, I saw that he was still asleep. When I asked him about the dingoes in the morning, he said he couldn't remember a thing about it.

We would stay at Mt Elliott for a few days at a time, and return to town each week after we were paid our wages. One night, as I was sitting in the Mitchell cafe around midnight, I was joined by my cousin Bodge Burns. We finished the carton together. I was drunk, and I don't think Bodge was much better. Anyway, we felt like a bit of excitement, and decided to break into the newsagent's. We climbed on the roof, broke a couple of louvres, and jumped down inside the shop. Bodge and I took anything we saw, filling two cardboard boxes with comics, magazines, tapes, and an assortment of other loot. Then we looked for a place to hide the stuff. We decided to push it up an old drain pipe, which turned out to be a dumb move in the end, since it was raining heavily that night. It was about five o'clock in the morning when I walked home.

Next day I felt terrible, and when I remembered what I'd done, I felt even worse. I wished to Christ it was all just a dream. I had never stolen anything in my life. When I put my hand in my pants pocket, I still had $120 there out of my wages – I could have bought all that stuff! I really did regret that episode. I'd always been honest up till then. Once, on my way to school – I was in grade seven – I'd picked up a purse with over $200 in it. Later that day, the purse was returned to its owner, a lady with five children, who really needed that money. She gave me five dollars reward, which meant a great deal to me.

I sat at home, just waiting for the police to pick me up. I waited two days. The rain finally cleared out the drainpipe where Bodge and I had hidden the two boxes. Someone found all the stolen goods and reported it to the police, who soon tracked us down. Bodge and I went to court and received a fine and eighteen months probation.

I didn't go back to work at Mt Elliott after this, because I was pretty ashamed of what I'd done. I was real sorry to leave that job. At the station, I'd fallen in love with a little brown-and-white mare named Shellie. Nowadays, whenever I see a horse as pretty as Shellie, I usually sit down to write a poem.

At this time, life at home was not happy. My mother had another man in her life and he lived with us. He called himself 'Weasey'. My father's death had broken everyone's heart and in the family we all experienced grief for the first time. My sisters took it tough, and my mother just fell to pieces. From that day she was never the same woman she had been when Dad was alive. Although I was sixteen, I felt somehow cheated by Weasey being in our house. He was okay when he was sober, but an old bastard when he was drunk. He and I locked horns more than once. When Weasey was drunk he would try to order everyone in the house about. At sixteen, I took orders from only one person in the family – my uncle, Johnny Dodd, whom I respected. I didn't understand how my mother could have betrayed us. This bloke Weasey wasn't fit to tie my Dad's shoelaces, let alone take his place. He never asked you to do anything – he just gave those orders. One day he ordered me to go downstairs and pick up the rubbish in the yard. I walked down to the yard … and I kept walking until I reached the cafe downtown. There was no way I would obey him.

In the end I moved my mattress and blankets outside and slept under a giant mulberry tree. I often felt a bit lonely in the middle of the night, so I'd go to the yard, bring up my horse Four X and tie him to the end of my bed with a tether rope. Whenever my old dog saw me getting out of bed to fetch Four X, he would start barking, and to stop everyone being woken up I'd get him from his kennel and tie him to my bed as well – much to his satisfaction.

One day, Weasey and I had a big blue downtown. He jumped out of his car and came at me swinging punches, so I gave him one on the jaw to keep him honest. He jumped back in the car and took off. I knew then it was time to leave home.

I moved into an old tin shed with my mate Alan Martin. We also had a boarder: Four X. Four X was only a young horse, and really hard to catch – so one night I decided to bring him into the shed alongside Alan and myself. Around midnight, I heard the sound of running water. 'Gee, Billboy, why don't you go out to the toilet?' Alan complained. – 'I thought it was you peeing on the floor,' I told Alan. When we turned around we found the culprit was Four X, of course. He wasn't toilet-trained, so we had to kick him out. It took me three days to find him after that, the cheeky mongrel. Our furniture in that tin shed consisted of two beds, four blankets, one mattress and a couch with a hole in it. When it rained most things got wet, but I enjoyed my stay there all the same.

It was now the end of 1982, and on New Year's Eve, Alan and I went out to celebrate with Michael Cambarngo in a little township nearby. During the evening, while we were drinking in a pub, I ran out of money and asked Michael for a loan of ten dollars. He told me that to get the ten dollars I had to go over and give a certain sheila a kiss for New Year. The only problem was that she was built like a brick shithouse – rumour had it that she had balls as well. However, I reckon ten dollars is worth about twenty dollars when you're broke, so I went over and gave her the kiss. She grabbed me in a bear hug and I disappeared into her big brown jacket. Then I tottered back to collect my ten dollars from Michael. He took one look at me and burst out laughing. 'Run your finger along the end of your nose,' he said. I wiped my nose – my finger came away red. At first I thought it was the girl's lipstick, but in fact my nose was bleeding. That was the hardest ten dollars I have ever earned.

A week later, I was at a party in Mitchell when Michael had a fight with a bloke known as 'Chocolate'. They both ended up on the ground, and I saw that Chocolate was putting in a bit of dirty fighting, so I picked up a plastic chair and donged him on the head. The chair just bounced off him and they kept on fighting. After it was all over, it was the chair that had come off worst; it had a broken leg. Michael is one of the toughest blokes I know.

Next day, I ran into Chocolate in the pub. He waited until I was fairly drunk before donging me on the head with a bar stool. My reaction was to throw my glass at Chocolate. The glass missed its target and hit this lady on the head – she had to get a few stitches, unfortunately. At closing time, it was her husband who ordered me outside for a fight. I was blind drunk as I shaped up. All I heard was the other bloke say: 'Come on, you bastard!' I felt his fists crashing into my face, then I went down hard on the bitumen and fell into the gutter. Just as I was getting up to my feet his boot came crashing into my stomach. One of my mates broke up the fight and carried me home. When I woke up in the old tin shed next morning there was dry blood on my pillow. The night before I'd been beaten physically; that morning I felt the pain of losing.

Too much grog. When I was sober I was a quiet bloke and never let people get to me, though I could pug on a bit. But unfortunately for me, most of the times I got into a fight I was drunk.

After the fight I packed up my gear and moved to Brisbane for a while. There I ran into my cousin, Margaret Finlay. One night Margaret and her mates showed me a few nightclubs, including a place called the Hacienda. Unknown to me, it was for gay people. I was just a country boy who never knew places like this existed. I was sitting down talking to one of the girls when I couldn't help noticing a guy wearing a suit and tie who kept staring at me. 'I bet that bloke over there is a police detective, and he's on to me for being in a club under-age,' I told Margaret. I felt a bit nervous – but the next time I looked at him, the 'detective' was kissing another bloke. I never hung around to see any more.

Later that night we had a second brush with the 'police', when we headed over to Musgrave Park. Margaret told me no one was allowed in the park after dark, so when we heard a siren that sounded like the police, we took off, running along the footpath. But it was only a big red fire truck that came speeding past us.

While I was in Brisbane, Margaret introduced me to a shy young Aboriginal girl from a small town called Murgon. Michelle Bligh was one of the prettiest girls I've ever seen. Looking at her in the pub that night, I thought she was even better looking than my beloved horses. During the next few months I saw a lot of

Michelle, until she went off to Tewantin to do a course. I decided to follow her there, and at Tewantin I met up with my cousin Bodge. A little later, Bodge and I set off to hitchhike to Gympie one night. It was really dark; even though Bodge was walking right beside me I couldn't see him. To tell the truth, I was shit scared. We made it safely to Gympie, however, and after staying there a while I went back to Brisbane and eventually returned to Mitchell.

When I got back home I never forgot that little shy girl called Michelle. Maybe I never will. I'm not sure whether I fell in love with her – but if not, then it was the closest I have ever been to falling in love. It was time and distance that tore us apart.

It was 24 September 1983 when my luck ran out. That day, the sun shone brightly, reflecting off my olive-coloured skin, and because it was so hot I decided to go for a swim in the river. My brother Peter came along too, and a few of my mates. Instead of checking how deep the water was, I dived in – and paid the penalty. Anyone who reads this and doesn't take five minutes to check a waterhole for depth, sticks and logs deserves to have their arse kicked with a size ten boot. It can give you a lot of unnecessary hassles, take it from me. So please think hard about it. Anyway, I dived into the water and my head struck the hard bottom of the river. My body crumbled with the impact and I sank to the bottom with a broken neck.

I lay under the water, unable to move. If my brother hadn't been there I might well have drowned. It was Peter who pulled me out of the Maranoa River and dragged me to the bank. I lay on my back and looked up into the blue sky. I saw an eagle hawk up there, flying high. It looked so free, it felt no pain up in that bright blue sky.

I thought to myself, if I could just get to my feet then I would be okay. One of my mates helped me to sit up, but when he let go of my head I felt a burning pain in the back of my neck. Oh boy, I felt sick with pain. So my mates laid me on the ground again. By this time my cousin, Wayne Dodd, had arrived. He rang the ambulance. Half an hour later I was on a stretcher in the back of the ambulance, heading towards Mitchell Hospital. When I arrived, the talk seemed to centre on a 'spinal unit' ... I had never heard of a spinal unit until that moment: To tell the truth, had I known that my neck was broken I would have been getting ready to die. In the bush I once saw a horse roll over backwards and hit its head on a rail. Its neck was broken and it died. After more discussion, it was decided that I would be transported by ambulance to the Princess Alexandra Hospital, in Brisbane.

24 September 1983, I screwed up for the last time.

6

During that 600 kilometre trip to Brisbane in the ambulance I was feeling really sick. I found it was getting harder to breathe – my breathing was getting shorter and quicker. By the time the ambulance reached Toowoomba I had blacked out. We finally arrived at the hospital in Brisbane about two o'clock in the morning.

When I dived into the river I had knocked myself out and had swallowed a lot of water. The doctor in Brisbane worked on me for over an hour, getting the water out of my lungs and clearing the muck off my chest.

Later that morning my mother received a phone call that told her she could lose her son. I was unconscious and in a bad way. Luckily for me, it was my fitness that helped to pull me through this little crisis. I was unconscious for three days. When I awoke, I was unsure about what had happened to me and where I was. I saw my mother and my sister Robyn standing there beside my bed. I took one look at them and without even saying 'Hello' I asked: 'Who won the America's Cup?' – 'Australia,' Robyn replied. – 'You little beauty,' I said. Even today, I can't understand how I could ask such a stupid question, as I have no interest in boat racing and the America's Cup was no exception. Maybe I had muddled it up with football! It was my eighteenth birthday, but I felt too sick to care. That day I became old enough to drink in a pub, and I didn't even feel I could be bothered to go for a beer. Something had to be wrong.

Meanwhile, Peter and my five sisters back in Mitchell were going through hell, waiting by the phone, answering it with caution, praying for good news, not bad. They were so relieved when I pulled through.

A few days later I was feeling a bit better, and I was moved out of the intensive care ward. As I had picked up an infection called golden staph, I was moved to an isolation ward. Then a few weeks later I was moved again, into the S7 ward. Here I found I was being hand-fed by a nurse. Two days later I found out the reason why.

Two doctors approached me, Dr Hill and Dr Davies. They had the task of informing me that I had a broken neck. Dr Hill also told me that I would never walk again. I would be confined to a wheelchair, not for a few months, not for a year, but for the rest of my life. Those words rang in my ears for a long time. In all my eighteen years I had never known tears to feel as cold as those that ran down my face. At that moment my reaction to what Dr Hill had told me was '*Oh no!* I'm better off dead.' At that time I didn't realise that I would be able to do the things I can do today. Sometimes we tend to think things are really worse than they are.

Deep down inside my heart, I knew that what Dr Hill had told me was correct, but for the moment I could not accept the idea of being in a wheelchair. I had to get used to the idea of trading my beloved horse Four X for that wheelchair.

When I broke my neck I lost all feeling and movement in my arms, chest and legs. These parts of my body were numb. Dr Hill told me that if I was to get any movement back in my arms, it would come during the first six weeks.

Each day I used to lie in bed with my arms spread out on two boards. I lay watching, waiting, praying – even though I did not really know how to pray. As the days passed I used to try and lift my arms off the boards. Each arm felt like it had a tonne weight placed on top of it. I never thought my arms were going to move. A few weeks later, when I thought all was lost, my arms actually made a mistake and moved. Now I found I could move them into my sides, but I never had enough movement to throw them back onto the boards.

Today I realise I am bloody lucky to be able to move my arms. I have only a patchy feeling in the top part of the arms, but although my fingers don't work, I still reckon I'm bloody lucky. Quadraplegics are the ones with courage: they cannot move their arms at all, but they never surrender the fight. So I can't whinge and can't complain. It doesn't matter how bad you think you are – if you open your eyes you will always find someone worse off than yourself.

I knew now, by the way my arms had moved, that what Dr Hill had told me was all true. As much as I did not want to believe it, I had to get used to the idea of being in a wheelchair, whether I liked it or not. I wondered how people would react when they saw my horse Four X replaced by that wheelchair. Time would tell.

For the next two months I continued to be fed by the nurses. I found it hard having the nurses do those things that once seemed so easy to do for myself. I really appreciated what they did for me – I reckon nurses are very special people.

I had a set of tongs put in each side of my head. Attached to the ends was a set of weights. The tongs were there to hold my neck straight while it mended. During these months in bed my skin became flaky and started to peel. The flaky skin made my face really itchy. I used to lie there putting up with the itchiness, and with my eyelashes falling into my eyes. While I was in hospital I was quiet and kept to myself; I was too shy to ask anyone for help. Apart from the flaky skin and the falling eyelashes I was feeling pretty good. Thirteen weeks later, Sister Pollock came around to release the tongs. Then I was allowed to have a shower, lying down on a trolley.

Before trying to sit up in a wheelchair, I was placed on my belly to try to lift my head off the pillow. I tried hard for five minutes. My head felt like a dead weight, but I refused to give in; I was really keen to get in that wheelchair. At my first attempt to sit in it, after two and a half months in bed, I saw stars and blacked out. I also found that I had no stomach muscles to hold me up. I had to be tied into the wheelchair with a strap. This made me feel a bit down in spirit; I thought I would be able to sit up without any problems. After the first few days in the wheelchair, the pain in the back of my neck was unbelievable. I was having trouble holding my head up; I never expected to feel so much pain. But each day I fought that pain and I found that the longer I sat up, the less the pain became.

Now it was time for my rehabilitation to begin. All the wheelchair patients had to be up and dressed and down in the gym by nine o'clock each morning. My physiotherapist was Diane Winterton, and my occupational therapist Sharon Steele. The time and effort they both put into rehabilitating me was terrific. They were easy to get on with, and the way they went about their work made things a hell of a lot easier for me.

Sharon Steele looked after my hands. With her help I had to learn to feed myself, clean my teeth, comb my hair, write and type – all with the use of splints. The splints were necessary, because feeling and movement never returned to my hands and fingers. When it came to feeding myself with a splint, I found there wasn't much food going into my mouth – but food going up my nose was a common occurrence. I'd start off feeling hungry but soon lost my appetite as I spilt more than I ate.

At first, I had to have someone to push me around in my wheelchair. Each day I exercised hard, hoping I would be able to push it along by myself. One day, after a good workout, my physio told me to have a go. I found I couldn't move it at all. I told my physio she had me pushing into the wind – I needed an excuse. Pushing my wheelchair along sounded such an easy thing to do – but here I was, unable to move it at all. After I whinged about pushing into the wind, my physio turned me around so that I was pushing into the opposite direction. She left me on a slope and my wheelchair rolled away by itself and crashed into the wall. I tried so hard to push that wheelchair, but I just couldn't make it go either backwards or forwards. I was in deep shit, bogged on a flat tiled floor.

A fortnight later, after exercising really hard, I found I could push the wheelchair over flat surfaces. Now my only trouble was trying to stop. I used to look down to see how fast I was going, and sometimes I'd look up again and find someone or something right in front of me. I had a few collisions, as I just couldn't move my arms or fingers to stop it quickly enough.

Every Friday, along with some of the other patients, I used to play sport. On the basketball court where we played some parts of the ground were uneven. When my wheelchair hit those spots it would roll away with me into the gutter. The first day I spent most of my time being retrieved from that gutter. But it was fun having a go. Today, I realise that winning isn't everything: having the courage to try is what counts. All these exercises kept me in good spirits.

By this time I knew all about the meaning of the words 'spinal unit'. It's a place where you are sent if you break your back or your neck. In 1983 the average age of patients admitted to the spinal unit at the Princess Alexandra Hospital was between seventeen and twenty-five. These people were the victims of falls, car crashes, sporting accidents (including a number of diving accidents), and accidents at work. Statistics showed that men outnumbered women. Young people admitted to the spinal unit often have their goals and dreams shattered when they are told they will never walk again. When they leave, six months later, it may be in a wheelchair. Each member of the spinal unit – doctors, physiotherapists, occupational physios, nurses – has a different job as they set about rehabilitating patients with spinal injuries. They aim to help and prepare them to go out and start living as normal a life as possible.

One day I was approached by Steve, another bloke in a wheelchair. Steve told me my diving accident was God's way of slowing me down. He said that God wanted me to lead a slower lifestyle. I reckoned that if God thought it was a good thing to live as slow a lifestyle as this, then I didn't want to know about it. 'Don't worry about anything – God is looking after us, He's Number One,' Steve said. To be honest, I don't agree with this: I reckon I am Number One, not God. I believe in myself. I'm not religious, I never have been, and I never will be. While I was in the PA spinal unit, I realised that if I never got in there and did all that hard work exercising my arms, but just sat waiting for God to come along and push my wheelchair, then I'd still be waiting six years later.

I've seen too many things in life go wrong to be able to believe in God. But I respect religious people and I realise they are entitled to their opinions.

As time passed, I realised my family couldn't afford to come down to Brisbane to spend much time with me while I was in the spinal unit. Mitchell was some six hundred kilometres away, and my sisters had young children at school. In any case, I preferred to be on my own, as sometimes my visitors would start crying when they came to see me. This used to piss me off – they made me feel like getting out of bed and kicking them in the arse. I had one regular visitor I was always pleased to see, a bloke called Graham Buckley, who came in each day after he finished work.

One day I received a pleasant surprise. The nurse came in and told me there was someone to see me, and in walked Mort Faddy, the policeman from Mitchell who had once told me that if I didn't shout him a beer when I turned eighteen, he would lock me up. 'You'd have to be one of the tightest blokes I know, Bill Dodd,' he told me now. 'See what happened when you didn't shout me that beer? You broke your neck.' He brought me a can of drink, a few packets of lollies and some chocolates. I've never forgotten him – I guess I owe him one.

I had my favourite nurses at the unit, including Crimmie, who was like a mother to me, and Andrea, young and good-looking. The first time we met I thought she was really cranky. I was lying in bed after a bad day and refused to take my tablets. Andrea just said:

'Take those tablets, ya little bugger.' In time I learned that she wasn't cranky at all – she had a great personality.

Another nurse in the unit was a bloke called John King. With Kingy you always heard him before you saw him. Another was a little dark fellow, Tony Pitt. When I first went to PA I was too scared to talk to anyone. I knew no one and distrusted practically everybody there. It was after I met Tony Pitt that I came out of my shell and started giving out a bit of cheek. Mick Weaver and Brian Sticher, two of the orderlies, also reduced the boredom for me a lot with their tricks and jokes. Sometimes they were a real torment to me. If I ever managed to put one over on them, they'd get even five minutes later. They'd maybe give me a cold shower, or put salt instead of sugar in my coffee.

After I'd been in the unit for five and a half months, I had to overcome one last obstacle: going out in public in my wheelchair. Sharon Steele, my occupational therapist, took me out shopping. I had imagined people would stare at me. Half an hour later we were on our way back to the hospital. No one seemed to have taken any notice of me – I was the one who had stared at some of the nice-looking girls in the store we visited.

Then Kingy and a couple of other orderlies decided to take some of the wheelchair patients for a night out. What better place to go to than a nearby pub. I looked forward to this – I hoped it would help me to get a bit of confidence in myself. My good mate Graham Buckley came along too. He held a glass of beer to my mouth so that I could have a drink, and after that I was ready to party. 'Find me a woman, Buckley!' I said jokingly. Only a bloke like Graham would be silly enough to take me seriously – it just proved what a good mate he was. There were these two sheilas in the pub, and Graham pushed me over to them and parked me right between them. Then he went back to the bar and just left me there.

I started talking to the girl on my left – she looked okay. She moved her chair closer to me and I thought, 'Aha, I'm set.' That was when Graham came back from the bar and proceeded to cut me out. All was not lost, however. The girl on my right moved her chair closer and started up a conversation with me. Boy, she was ugly, though. I realised she was the type who had probably been around more blocks than the postman. 'Get me out of here,' I told Graham. But he said, 'Just sit there, mate, I'm doing all right.' Then the girl on my right tried to put her arm around me, but I wouldn't let her – she had shoulders like a man, and I couldn't afford to break my neck twice. However, the more I drank the better looking she seemed to become. (That night I was nicknamed 'the pot screamer': drink one, spill one and give one away.) The only thing that saved me from this sheila in the end was ten o'clock closing time. Without thinking, I gave the girls my address at the hospital before leaving them.

Next morning, I woke up with a headache that would kill a horse and paralyse an elephant. Of all the nurses, it had to be Kingy who was on duty that day. He came into the room and said, 'How's lover boy this morning?' Gee, I copped heaps that day. A little later, as I was sitting outside in my wheelchair telling Crimmie how well-behaved I'd been last night, I heard Kingy yell out: 'Has anyone seen Billy Dodd? Tell him there are two girls here – they said they met him at the pub last night!' As soon as I heard this I took off in my wheelchair, and in my haste to get away I pushed myself over a hump in the doorway. That was the only time I ever managed to get over that bloody hump – quite an achievement. I soon found out, to my relief, that Kingy was bullshitting me. Seven years later, he still hasn't let me forget that night when I was almost led astray.

My last outing before I left PA was to a place on the outskirts of Brisbane known as O'Reilly's. This was arranged for a few of the wheelchair patients by the hospital. I don't think I've ever seen country as pretty as that around O'Reilly's. We used to sit out in front of the guest cabins and flocks of brightly coloured parrots would appear. We were given birdseed to feed them. The parrots would fly down and sit in your lap or on top of your head. To tell the truth I couldn't stand those birds – I just sat there, stiff as a board, cursing them under my breath. I mean, they'd fly down, pick up the birdseed, shit on your head and fly away.

The people who ran O'Reilly's were very kind. They were so interested in me, a complete stranger to them. I really enjoyed my few short days' holiday there.

I had now completed my six months at the Princess Alexandra spinal unit. It had been tough. Now it was time to leave the hospital and move on.

7

After my rehabilitation at PA, I was put on a plane and flown to Roma. (The only other flight I'd ever experienced was when I went from Katherine to Auvergne station – all that now seemed like another world to me.) I was booked to stay at a nursing home called Westhaven, because there was nowhere in Mitchell with suitable facilities for a quadraplegic. I knew that Westhaven was really a nursing home for old people.

I arrived there in April 1984. I felt a bit scared, and I found that Westhaven was very different to the way I'd pictured it in my mind. That first night I ate supper in the dining room all by myself. I felt a real stranger; for the first time in my life I was really alone. Westhaven was to be the place I called 'home' for the next five years and eight months. The next youngest patient to me was aged about fifty.

I was eighteen, and apart from the fact that I was in a wheelchair I now felt as fit as a fiddle. When I arrived at Westhaven I still hadn't accepted being confined to my wheelchair; I still thought I could go out partying all night. I used to get away with quite a lot; sometimes I did go out until the early hours of the morning. I would have been in strife if I'd done that in Brisbane. I guess I was still as mad as a cut snake.

Gradually I got used to the other people at Westhaven, and came to understand that many elderly folk tend to become a bit confused, with loss of memory. Had I come to Westhaven just as a visitor, I might have thought differently – but in almost six years I learned a lot. Even so, some of the things that happened there I found hard to believe. There were about four people I could have a decent conversation with. It was really a pretty sad place; some of the patients would quickly slide downhill and chuck it in after they arrived there. You couldn't afford to get too close or take a liking to any of those old people. If I hadn't had the help of some very sympathetic nurses I don't think I could have handled my long stay there too well.

I recall that soon after I arrived I was sitting outside my room one day, talking to Sister Ramage, when this old lady came walking towards us with no clothes on. I went as red as a beetroot – no matter where I looked she seemed to be there, and in the end I ducked outside.

Another time, as I was eating lunch in the dining room with my back turned to the door, a big hand came out of nowhere and I watched a potato disappear off my plate. The hand belonged to a lady called Nell, who stuffed the potato in her mouth and took off. I learned a valuable lesson that day: never eat with your back to the door. (It was a lesson I'd already learned in that other world, Auvergne, when we were drafting wild bullocks.)

Then there was Connie, another patient. She was a real nice lady, always trying to help others. Sometimes, as I made my way in my wheelchair along the hallway, Connie would come over and start pushing me. She'd push me until the wheels got stuck against a wall or some other barrier, then take off and leave me stranded. For a joke, one of the nurses told Connie I ran the taxi service in Roma, and after that she used to come up to me and say: 'I'll give you two shillings to take me home.'

My hair grew really long while I was at Westhaven. Once, as I was sitting in my room doing a crossword puzzle, Connie and two other old ladies walked past my door. They were looking for the toilet, having forgetten where it was. 'Don't worry,' Connie told the other two ladies, 'I'll ask the nice little lady in this room where it is.' And one morning, as I was being wheeled to the shower without a shirt on, Connie called out that she was pretty disgusted that I wasn't wearing a bra. Believe it or not, I took a real liking to Connie.

Another Westhaven patient was an old fellow named Tom. He was known as the 'pug' of Westhaven. He wouldn't take a backward step from anyone, and carved quite a reputation. I found it safer to keep out of his way. One day I saw Tom throw a left hook at one of the nurses, and even though it missed, she fell over with fright. Poor old Tom's reputation received a setback, however, when he was ko'd by another patient, Bronc.

But Tom had a bit of fight, a bit of spirit and plenty of character.

One of my mates was a little dark lady, Vera. I now had two twelve-volt batteries on the back of my wheelchair which made it much easier to get along. The first time I met Vera was at lunch one day. A nurse was wheeling over a small table for my meal when it clipped the top of the joystick I used to manoeuvre the chair. I had forgotten to press the on/off button, and the chair promptly went into reverse and came to a halt right on poor old Vera's foot. Suddenly I heard this voice from behind me: 'Get off my foot, you bloody bugger!' Who got the bigger fright, Vera or myself, I don't know. I managed to get the heavy wheelchair off her foot and her reaction was straightforward: she clipped me under the ear. The nurse thought it was a great joke. Vera used to tell me that Banjo Paterson was her son, and she used to collect cigarette lighters – in fact, she would enter anyone's room and take anything that wasn't nailed down. The sad part was that poor old Vera didn't know she was doing this; for her it was just part of growing old. While I was at Westhaven I was only too aware that one day I might end up like Vera. It made me think long and hard. One night I was lying in bed watching television when Vera came in and picked up the water jug on my bedside table. I plucked up a bit of courage and said, 'Don't take that jug, Vera, bring it back here.' She brought it back all right – and threw the water all over me. From that day, Vera had me bluffed.

Annie was a patient who had a bad habit of getting into other people's beds, even if they were still in them. Once, as I was lying in bed watching the Balmain Tigers play a match on TV, Annie came into my room and started to climb into bed with me. Somehow I managed to persuade her to go. I was very glad I didn't have to sing out to one of the nurses – boy, I would have copped heaps. As it was, Annie went away, taking one of my pillows with her. Unfortunately it had been propping me up so that I was able to see the TV set. Being a real keen Balmain supporter, I was pissed off at missing the rest of the match.

I liked to lie out in the sun sometimes, facedown on a mattress. I would lie there with a sheet over my head. One day I felt liquid coming through the sheet and running down the side of my face. 'One of the old buggers is peeing on me!' was my first awful thought. For someone who couldn't move his fingers, I had that sheet off my face in a real hurry ... to find a nurse standing there with a grin on her face and a garden hose in one hand. I was one relieved Murri: a bit of clean water never hurt anyone.

At Westhaven I had some good times and a few that weren't so good, but no matter how hard things got, I always managed to keep it together. Each morning after my shower I used to go back to bed to exercise for at least one and a half hours. This helped me to get rid of a lot of frustration and to feel better in myself. But if I was feeling really down I used to keep it bottled up inside. Some days

I got so pissed off that I didn't want to talk to anyone. But today I can look back at the good times and laugh.

Most of the nurses at Westhaven treated me really well, and helped me to sort out my problems. I still keep in touch with some of them, and every year I get a birthday card from the staff. I know that I made a few enemies at Westhaven, too. Soon after I arrived, I was pushing my wheelchair along the hallway when I heard one of the wardsmen say: 'I don't know why they sent him, he doesn't belong here.' At that moment I wanted to be at the nursing home about as much as that wardsman wanted me there. It doesn't matter who, how or what you are, you'll always find people who will put you down and try to make life hard for you. There was also one nursing sister who gave me a hard time at Westhaven. She had that habit of ordering me to do something rather than asking me – rather like Weasey, on whose account I had left home. I had to stand up to that nurse, and one day I finally told her, very politely, to piss off and get out of my room. She reported me to the matron, but it was worth it, as she laid off me for a while after that.

While I was at Westhaven I had a job as a clerical assistant with the Community Youth Support Scheme and went each weekday to the centre in Roma. My bosses were two senior project officers, Ken Skinner and Bernadette Clarke. The main role of the CYSS was to train young people and hopefully find them full-time employment. My job was to answer the phone and also to take a few of the trainees through a word-processing course on the computer. I liked the people I worked with and they were very helpful to me. This job was really the best thing that ever happened to me – it made me realise there was more to life than doing crosswords and watching videos.

Occasionally I would persuade a nurse to let me go outside the home in my electric wheelchair. One day I was just two blocks away when I hit a patch of sand and sank right down into it. I sat there helpless, and thought about signalling to one of the cars driving past and asking someone to pull me up and push me out of the sand. I watched one car come up and thought, 'I'll signal this driver', then I thought, 'No! I'll sing out to the next one instead' … But I wasn't game to sing out to anyone. Even when the postman came by on his motorbike I found I was lost for words. Then a nurse appeared on her way to lunch. I did sing out to her, and I felt a real mug as I asked her to push me out of that sand. It felt somehow shameful to get bogged like that. A car, fair enough – but not a wheelchair! Another time I got bogged on a wet track. I'd gone out at six o'clock in the evening and two hours later I was still in the same place. I was scared of the dark, but by the time a nurse found me I was almost asleep.

I guess that falling out of my wheelchair was just as bad as falling off a horse. I'd fallen off plenty of horses in my time. After my accident, I remember thinking that I never imagined I would break my neck diving into a river – something I had done so many times before. Something so simple. To date, I've fallen out of my wheelchair eight times in about seven years. My first fall was in Mitchell. It happened when I went home for a weekend. I met one of my mates who was drunk, and he came over and tried to tackle me – he hit me around my neck and down I went. Well, if you hang around people who drink I guess you sometimes pay the penalty.

My second and third times were when I got tipped out of the back of my chair twice in the space of one hour. The fourth time, I was at a twenty-first birthday celebration out in the country. This girl was pushing me backwards, using my knees to steer, but as we reversed we hit a big hole and my chair tipped over backwards.

The fifth time was at a bachelor and spinsters' ball, when I got rolled going down some steps. I saw the steps for the first time as I landed arse-up at the bottom. The sixth time I was sober. I was being lifted into bed by a nurse and a wardsman. The nurse lifted my legs before the wardsman lifted the upper half of my body, so that all the weight went to the top of the wheelchair and it toppled over backwards.

My seventh fall happened one day when I was having a few drinks with some mates. I was parked on a bit of a slope outside the pub. Everything was going well until I came to the last drop of beer in my can. When I tipped back my head my wheelchair reared backwards just like a mad horse. My head hit the cement, but I was okay. The eighth time I was partying at the nurses' quarters when I just fell out of my chair in a beautiful forwards motion.

★

I never thought I would leave Westhaven to come back and live in Mitchell. I have nine nephews and nieces. While I was in Roma I never went home to Mitchell very often, so that I was more or less a complete stranger to them – except for my eldest sister's kids, Damon and Trent. Narelle, my sister, was living in Roma with a real nice bloke, Danny Halpin.

Damon is eleven now, and one of the quietest and best mannered children I know. When Narelle was still living in Mitchell, and before I broke my neck, I used to babysit Damon for her. I recall the first time I ever changed a nappy. I ran around in circles a few times, and found that the nappy I'd put on kept coming off. I didn't realise that I'd put it on back to front. Finally I decided to wrap insulation tape around and around it. The nappy stayed on all right – but it didn't want to come off.

Trent, at nine, is a funny little fellow and a real outlaw. One day when he was giving his mother cheek, he pushed her too far. Narelle took a thong off one foot to flog him. When Trent saw the size of his mother's thong, he yelled out: 'Wait on, Mum, wait on!' Narelle asked him what was wrong. Trent replied: 'Could you please use my thong – it's smaller.'

One of my nieces, a pretty little baby girl called Shannon, died of cot death syndrome when she was five months. I had only seen her twice during her short lifetime. It was Shannon's death that really made me want to leave Westhaven.

On 29 June 1989 I returned to Mitchell. In a way

I was sorry to leave Westhaven, in another way I was glad to get out. I looked out of the window of my room for the last time. It had been my home for five years and eight months. In that room I had shed a few tears and had a few laughs. I came into Westhaven a boy; I left that place a man. I think I matured a bit as I got older. I will never forget Westhaven nursing home, nor some of the mates I made there. Westhaven: a little place on top of a hill in Roma.

8

So I came back to live in Mitchell, my home town. A small place that today has five pubs and a population of 1212. To begin with, I lived with my brother Peter and my sister Michelle. (Weasey had died a few years ago, and my mother now lives with Michelle.) Since I moved back home I have a lot more freedom and I see much more of my mates. They weren't real sure about coming to see me while I was in a nursing home.

One of the first things that happened was that I made an enemy: my sister's white cat, Pitta Pat. It began one night when I was just dozing off to sleep – it was about ten o'clock. Something disturbed me: I opened my eyes and came face to face with Pitta Pat, who was sitting on my chest. I can't move my arms much when I'm lying down, and when I tried to make the cat get off me she grabbed hold of one arm and started scratching and clawing. I had to call out for Michelle to come and back me up. A bit embarrassing, to be beaten by a cat!

A few nights later I had another run-in with Pitta Pat. This time it was around eleven. Lying in bed, I heard the cat enter my room and jump up on the desk. On top of the desk I have a telephone with numbers dialled into the memory function, so that when I want to ring up someone, all I have to do is press one button. After the number is automatically dialled the phone works like an intercom, so that I don't have to pick up the handpiece to talk or listen to whoever it is at the other end of the line. Somehow the cat walked over the top of my phone and must have pressed one of the buttons. Sudenly I heard this voice say loud and clear: 'Hello, this is the Roma fire brigade.' A mate of mine was in the fire brigade, and that was why the number was dialled in there. I lay in bed not knowing whether to reply or keep quiet. I mean, if I said: 'Sorry, but it was a cat that rang you up' who would believe me? They'd probably want to put me in a strait jacket and send a little white truck to take me away.

I am sure Pitta Pat knows she can put it over me. One day as I was sitting typing this story, she jumped on my desk. Then she came over and sat on the keyboard. When I tried to go on typing, she grabbed my arm and started to bite. Like a real wimp, I had to sing out to Peter to come and kick Pitta out of my room. I don't think Pitta really likes Murries – well, not this one, anyway.

Since coming home, I miss my horse Four X and my faithful dog, Mungrel. I never had a chance to see Mungrel again after I left the PA spinal unit, as he was with my horse out in the bush, and now he is dead.

As I sit in my room, I look at my sports trophies displayed on the cabinet. I took up boxing at thirteen – I never had much style, but I could hit hard and I also had a hard head, which enabled me both to take and to give out a hiding. Those boxing and football trophies meant a lot to me: they were an indication that I was playing well, and winning. Today they no longer mean anything to me. When this book is completed and launched, I can bury my memories of sport. Instead, I hope to write.

For a long time my football memories were pretty sad for me. When I came home from PA I went to the football in my wheelchair for the first time since my accident. As I watched the Mitchell Magpies run onto the field I felt real low and down in spirit. If things hadn't turned out the way they did, I knew I could have been running onto that field. I recalled the week just before my accident, when I played with the Magpies and we won the Grand Final. I felt pretty helpless, sitting in my wheelchair. Ten minutes later I'd seen enough of the game and headed for the bar. But now, with each year that goes by, I find it easier to go to the football. Today, I don't even notice that I'm sitting in my wheelchair as I watch the game.

In 1989 I was presented with a beautiful football jacket. It was the players who put in to get me this jacket. It just goes to show that they still believe in me, as I do in them. Words on paper cannot tell how much I appreciate this jacket. When people do something like this it makes things a hell of a lot easier for me. The people in Mitchell also put in to buy me an electric typewriter. For me, life was always a bit of a struggle and if I wanted anything I had to battle for it. I never thought I would get a typewriter given to me. Although I needed one, I wasn't game to ask anyone to help me out. Now I sit here using that typewriter with a special splint on one finger.

Since coming home I've become a lot closer to my nephews and nieces in Mitchell. Anne is the second eldest of my five sisters. She lives with a fellow called Robert Doyle and they have two lovely children, Cheyne and Kym. Cheyne is four and fairly shy until she gets to know you. Kym is three and really cute. Her look of innocence gets her out of a lot of trouble.

My sister Robyn has three children – Sharna, Daniel and Dennii. Sharna is six, a great little mate and good company. One day Sharna's grandmother asked her: 'What are you going to do when I go up to heaven?' Sharna looked at her grandmother, shook her head and answered: 'Don't worry, Nan, I'll be there beside you.' Another day, one of Sharna's teeth fell out, so she put it in a glass for the tooth fairy to come along. That night, some of my mates came to the house and sat up all night partying on. Next morning, Sharna went to the glass to get the money the tooth fairy would have left in exchange for the tooth. But the tooth was still in the glass and there was no money. 'Nan,' she complained to her grandmother, 'those noisy mongrels sat up all night drinking – they must have scared the tooth fairy away.'

Daniel is two and a nice-looking kid. He's mad on Santa Claus. One day we were watching television when Santa came on the screen. He walked over to a pretty lady who was also in the picture and Daniel said: 'Look, Mum, there's Santa and Mrs Claus!' Later that day, as we were on our way downtown, a helicopter flew over and Daniel reckoned that was Santa Claus going home for a rest. One thing I like about Daniel is that he can give as good as he gets. And he always shares with you. One time he had a packet of chips and I asked him to give me one. 'No,' he said. 'Why not?' I asked, surprised. 'Say "please", Uncle Bill, then you can have a chip,' he told me.

Dennii is five months old and when he grows up a bit, with Daniel around, I guess they'll be a pair of outlaws together.

Michelle, my fourth eldest sister, has two kids, Teeghan and Jayde. They now live in Morven with their father. Teeghan is six and his brother Jayde is five. Jayde and I share the same birthday: when I turned twenty-one, Jayde was one year old. Each afternoon after school, those two boys used to run up the road to do some chores for an old bloke they knew. He used to pay them their 'wages' every Friday. Sometimes, during the week the boys would get sidetracked and play with their mates instead. One Friday they were on their way to their chores when they ran into some of their mates, who wanted them to play. 'Let's play,' Teeghan said, but Jayde shook his head. 'Bugger you, Teeghan, you can stop and play but I'm going to work – it's pay day.'

My brother Peter is twenty now. I don't think brothers come much better than Peter. He knows his own mind, doesn't care too much about other people's opinions and doesn't let people get to him.

Last but not least is my sixteen-year-old sister, Donna, the youngest in our family. She often gives me a hand when I do leatherwork. Donna is really patient with me, and sometimes she needs to be.

Today I really believe in my sisters. Once, when I came from Westhaven to stay in Mitchell for the weekend, I found that Peter was out, so he couldn't help to lift me out of the car into my wheelchair. My sisters came out to greet me and said they'd lift me out instead. I was a bit of a male chauvinist at that time and told them they wouldn't be strong enough. Most of the men who lifted me whinged about how heavy I was. Without a word, Michelle and Robyn took charge. Robyn grabbed me under the shoulders and Michelle took my legs, and that lift was as good as any I had known. Robyn never said a word, just looked at me as if to say – 'Now will you bloody shut up.'

Before my accident, I guess I never really appreciated my sisters as much as I do today. I have to depend on them a lot. Seven years ago I would never have dreamed that I would write this sentence, but if one of our family had to end up with a broken neck, I'm glad it was me and not one of my sisters or Peter, for they don't deserve to be hurt in any way.

I have had a lot of time to look back over my life and think about myself, and without too many regrets I realise where I went wrong from time to time. I was young and wild. If my father had still been alive, then I reckon there would have been no way I would have been going out at night, drinking. I know I would have received a few more kicks up the arse. I would have obeyed my father because I respected him more than I've ever respected anyone else.

It's really great to have got to know my nieces and nephews so well. They are curious about me and ask a lot of questions. I try to explain things to them. For instance, I can't feel my bladder, so I don't know when I'm urinating. When I do a pee, it runs down a tube into a drainage bag with a tap which you turn to empty it. One day I tucked the tap neatly into my sock, not realising that the nurse who visits me every day had forgotten to turn it off. The result was that I peed into my boot. When something like that happens, all you can do is smile. (The kids thought it was a great joke.) Life is too short to let a little thing like that worry you. Another day, I was lying in bed when young Daniel came into my room. He looked at the drainage bag and remarked: 'Orange cordial!' All my nieces and nephews give me a bit of help, a lot of laughs and a bit of strength as life goes on.

9

I don't think we know who our real mates are until the chips are well and truly down. I've found that a real mate will stick by you, no matter what, while others find they just haven't got time for you any more. Even today I'm not really sure what I mean when I call someone 'mate', but all the people I write about in this chapter I think of as my mates.

At school, I had five people I called 'mates'. In those days, a mate was someone who would back you up in a fight, even if you both knew you'd be beaten. Ten years later I still have four of those mates: Alan Martin ('Chong'), Michael Cambarngo, David Nixon and Graham Buckley. Chong and I were like brothers – we more or less grew up together. If I got into strife, Chong was never far away. Back in 1982, Graham and I had a fist fight and I put him into hospital with concussion. These days, he jokes about that. A year later, in Brisbane, it was Graham who came every afternoon when he'd finished work to visit me in the spinal unit at PA.

Soon after I arrived at Westhaven, I went to watch

Mitchell play the Wattles in Roma. It was a very hot day and I was sitting in the car when I was approached by a young bloke who introduced himself to me as Greg Doyle. He was living with my cousin, Robyn Finlay, in Mitchell, and he invited me to stay with them one weekend, an offer I took up later on. Greg was a top bloke. When he was in Roma he'd always call in to see if I wanted to go to the football, or visit Mitchell for a few days. One day, as Greg and I were having a yarn, he told me he had cancer. The doctors had given him twelve months to live. In spite of this, he never changed – he kept on coming to see me. As time passed, I could tell he had trouble keeping up with the other blokes when we went out to the pub; sometimes he'd have to go home as he wasn't feeling too good. Greg Doyle was someone really special. He never whinged or complained, even though he knew he was dying.

One night at Westhaven, my sister Narelle came to tell me that one of my five schoolmates, Adrian Finlay, had been killed in a car accident. The car in which he was a passenger left the road and turned over. He was twenty-one. On 25 July 1987, I lost a great mate who could make you laugh even when times were tough.

Early the next year I received a telephone call and learned that Greg Doyle had passed away. Although I knew he had cancer, somehow I had never really believed he would die – not a young bloke of twenty-one, who had done so much for me. After I heard this news I went outside and disappeared into the night for a while.

If ever I needed a mate it was then. Tears ran down my cheeks as I thought about the good times we'd had. As the loneliness of the night closed in, I didn't want to go back to my room – I just wanted to be alone. I was usually a bit frightened about being outside by myself in the wheelchair in the dark. But that night I didn't care.

One thing that the deaths of Greg and Adrian proved to me was that I did have a heart that can bleed and I do care about other people. When I was sixteen, I wasn't sure about that. I think it has taken life in a wheelchair for me to appreciate others, and I seem to have learned to get closer to people. There's a different view from a wheelchair.

Back in Roma, I had a group of mates who would take me to the disco or the football, the drive-in, or for a seafood meal. We even went to the races, and once two of them strapped me in a life jacket and conned me into going for a swim in the nurses' pool at Westhaven. I used to go partying with the nurses – they were a lot of fun, and I was always sorry when those I got to know well completed their twelve months' training and moved on.

Taking me around involves lifting me in and out of a car and stowing my wheelchair in the boot. I don't think it would matter to my mates in Mitchell if the only way I could get around was by elephant: they'd still lift me into the car, then put the elephant in the boot. Once two of my mates lifted me in my wheelchair up the steps of the football grandstand so that I wouldn't get rained on.

Two girls I got to know in Roma are Donna Clifford and Lisa Aspinall. Donna was doing work experience at Westhaven – she was sixteen when I first met her. I was sitting in the sun in my wheelchair when she came over and started talking to me. Suddenly a gust of wind blew her skirt up a bit too high. Poor kid, I thought to myself, and tried to talk to her as though nothing had happened. But I found the words wouldn't come out – all I could do was laugh. Donna, a bit embarrassed, turned red and took off. That was the only time I've ever seen her lost for words. She's a great mate, and whenever I see her, I remind her of that incident.

I met a girl named Lisa Aspinall at a party in Roma. As I was talking to her, the beer I was drinking ran out and I decided to go back to Westhaven. 'You can't go yet,' Lisa said. 'I know where I can get another beer.' Ten minutes later she came back with a stubby – she had gone home to get it. 'I took one of Dad's beers out of the fridge,' she said. She had left him a note that said – 'Dear Dad, I took one beer for Billy Dodd. Love, Lisa.'

I drank that stubby, then Lisa went home for another beer and left another note –

'Dear Dad, I took one more beer for Billy Dodd. Love, Lisa.'

After drinking that one, she got me a third and left one more note –

'Dear Dad, I took one more beer for Billy Dodd. Love, Lisa.'

After three beers I did go home. About a week later,

I met a new wardsman at Westhaven. His name was Rex. When he came in to lift me out of bed and put me in the shower chair, the nurse introduced us. 'Rex, this is Billy Dodd,' she said.

'Billy Dodd!' Rex exclaimed. 'You're the bloke who drank my beers!' He told me how he'd woken up one morning to find those three notes on his fridge door.

Two of the most faithful mates I've ever had would have to be my faithful horse Four X and my blue cattle dog, Mungrel.

Mungrel got himself into a lot of mischief. One day I was riding a young horse that kept taking off and kicking up. I wondered what was wrong, and as I rode along I looked at the shadow of me and the horse – I thought maybe a loose strap was hitting him under the belly. Then I noticed another shadow – my dog. He was coming in all the time and biting the horse on one of its hind legs. 'You're nothing but a mongrel, dog!' I sang out to him – and that was how he got his name.

For three years Mungrel and I grew up together. Some mornings, if I was still asleep when my brother Peter got up, he would let Mungrel off his chain, and then my dog would come upstairs to wake me up. Like the rogue he was, he'd come to the top of the stairs and look around to see if my mother was there – he wasn't really allowed indoors. If all was clear, he'd run into my room and jump all over me. Hopefully, he'd make it outside again before my mum arrived with the broom.

One day I needed Mungrel's help. I was seventeen,

and having a real bit of trouble with our local postman, who was going out with one of my sisters. I was seventeen and he was twenty, and if we'd had a punch-up I knew I would have come off worst. A few days after a bad argument with him, I watched as he pedalled along on his bike, delivering the mail. I decided to let Mungrel off the chain, and as the postman approached our mailbox I sooled the dog onto old mate. The postie scored a fast lap up the road and I gave Mungrel a piece of steak and a pat on the head for a job well done.

The day of my accident was the last time I saw my faithful blue cattle dog. One of my mates took my horse and dog into the bush to look after them, and when I finally came back to Mitchell, over six years later, he told me my dog had passed away.

The last mate I want to talk about is a fellow called Chris Martin, known as 'Bunny'. Ever since I've been in a wheelchair, Bunny has been my best mate. He's a quiet bloke and nothing seems to worry him. He has done a lot for me and takes me to lots of places. This bloke wouldn't say twenty words a day when he's sober, but like me he makes up for it when he's had a few beers.

In February 1990 I decided to go to Cairns to see my favourite cousin, Deana. My sister Donna, cousin Dearne, Bunny and myself all went off together. We spent a week at Ipswich on the way, staying with some relatives, two weeks in Cairns, then went back to Ipswich for another week. During our first stay at Ipswich, Bunny and I drank beer most of the time. One night, three of my cousins took Bunny to a disco. My cousins made it home all right, but they lost poor old Bunny somewhere. Next day we discovered that Bunny had got himself locked up by the law and spent the night in the clink. By the fifth night in Ipswich, the grog began to take its toll on Bunny. At midnight, when everyone else was asleep, he jumped off his bed and tried to pick up the big television set. His grunting and groaning woke up a fellow called David. 'What d'you think you're doing, Bunny?' he asked. – 'No worries, mate,' Bunny replied, 'I'm just lifting Bill into his wheelchair so we can go down the pub.'

Next day, as we travelled by train to Cairns, Bunny and I were two sick boys. We were two days and a night on the train, and when we got to Cairns we spent a lot more time sober.

We enjoyed ourselves in Cairns, and after two weeks it was time to leave. We had to catch the train at seven o'clock on Saturday morning, and the night before we all went to a nightclub. Next morning, one of the girls in the house where we were staying told us it was six o'clock, so we had one hour to get ready and be at the train station. Dearne came in to help me, and then I looked at the clock on the wall ... its hands were pointing to seven. I thought it must be daylight saving, but in fact it *was* seven and we'd missed the train. However, we made it back to Brisbane and stayed in Ipswich for another week before catching the bus back to Mitchell.

Not everyone I knew turned out to be a good mate. Like I said at the beginning of this chapter, we don't know who our real mates are until the chips are down. One bloke who disappointed me was Scoob. He was from Mitchell, and I ran into him in Brisbane one night. I was seventeen at the time. We went to a disco together one night. On our way home we found ourselves walking along behind a bloke who was really bandy-legged. 'Hey, cowboy, where's your horse?' I called out to him. The bloke swung around, saw Scoob and told him to put his fists up. 'Wait until I take my shirt off,' Scoob said. When the shirt was off the other bloke said, 'Come on, then.' Scoob replied, 'Wait until I get my shoes off.' – 'Okay, let's fight,' the bloke said when this was done. – 'Wait until I take off my socks,' Scoob said. I thought, if Scoob keeps this up it could get a bit embarrassing. I said, 'Do you want me to fight him for you, Scoob?' He replied, 'God, I thought you'd never ask.' I threw a couple of punches and the bloke took off.

Before my accident, Scoob seemed a good mate, but afterwards I realise all he'd wanted was for me to fight his battles. I was sitting in my wheelchair in the pub in Mitchell one day and saw Scoob at the bar. He couldn't even walk over to say 'good-day'. But I guess he wasn't a real mate in the first place.

My other mates haven't let me down in any way. There are heaps of others I haven't mentioned here – if I went through all the people who have helped me out in different ways, I'd run out of paper. The help and understanding I've had from people in Mitchell and Roma has been invaluable. For all those who've helped me – whether it's been lifting me up stairs or moving a stool so that I could get a bit closer to the bar, all I can say is: thanks, I do appreciate it.

10

At the time of my accident, seven years ago, I never thought I would come to terms with being a quadraplegic in a wheelchair. I heard the doctor say that I was paralysed from the lower part of my chest down and would have to go around in a wheelchair for the rest of my life – but for a while I was living in hopes that maybe the doctor was wrong, and one day I might walk again. I reckoned that if I saw a good-looking girl or a bucket of booglies (crayfish) then I'd walk. I saw both, and I'm still in my wheelchair.

My change of attitude began the day I started exercising in the spinal unit at PA. That was when my sense of hopelessness began to disappear. I thought then that I had accepted my fate mentally, but in my dreams it was a different story. I reckon the first time I pictured myself in a dream as being in a wheelchair, instead of walking up a road, that was a fair indication that I had accepted things not only physically, but in my mind as well.

I am a bit of a dreamer. One time I dreamt I was pushing myself in my wheelchair down to the Mitchell showgrounds to watch a game of football, with a sixpack of stubbies under my arm. On my way I lost the pack, so I turned around to try to track it down. Then I saw a police car under a big bottle tree, with two policemen inside it. When I went over to see if they could help me, I found they were drinking a sixpack of stubbies ... At that moment I seemed to be woken up by some idiot yelling out: 'You bastards, you're drinking my sixpack of stubbies!' It was my own voice I heard.

Being paralysed has been a real challenge for me. I have to rely so much on other people. Since coming home to live in Mitchell, I have to wait each morning until the girls are ready to shower me. This is frustrating; it's impossible to get into a routine and they shower me at different times each day. At Westhaven, it usually happened at the same time every morning. And at home I do miss the wardsmen who used to lift me in and out of my wheelchair. At home, my sisters do this job.

I have experienced feelings of disappointment, despair, frustration and desparation. I guess there has even been a time for tears, which I am unashamed to mention. But I have found that the more time I've spent in my wheelchair, the easier things have become.

As I sit here typing, it is the happiest time for me since I broke my neck. As I type, my three-year-old nephew Daniel is beside me. I used to think Daniel was a true blue Balmain supporter in Sydney's rugby league. When he sees me he says: 'Uncle Bill, Balmain are the best.' So you give him a couple of dollars for being a good mate. But when Daniel sees my brother Peter, who is a Gold Coast supporter, he says: 'Peter, the Gold Coast are the best, hey.' Then Daniel will see David Nixon, an Illawarra supporter. 'David, Illawarra are the best,' he'll say. Perhaps you could say he's just being diplomatic.

The splint I use has been made especially for typing. It is moulded to fit on my first finger, with a rubber stopper on the end which enables me to press the typewriter keys. Using one finger, it takes me about two hours to type a page. It comes along slowly but surely. I enjoy doing things for myself.

If you are quadraplegic you have to accept things, get in there and have a go. You don't let the wheelchair get in your way; if you want to do something badly enough, then you'll do it. My goal for the past seven years was to go to Cairns, which I did. My three goals for the next seven years are: to go to the horse races at Doomben, in Brisbane; to go to the Gabba to watch Queensland play a shield match in cricket; and to visit the Hall of Fame at Longreach. I set goals that are reachable. If you sit down and start feeling sorry for yourself, being negative, then you're no bloody good to anyone. You are only young once and life waits for no man, woman or child. Like the *Phantom* comics say, in the jungle the strong survive.

During the past seven years I reckon I've done more good for myself than I did in my whole life before 24 September 1983. I've changed my ways because I had no other choice. If I hadn't broken my neck, I often wonder where I'd be today.

In a way, I guess I was unlucky to have met my accident diving into a creek. If I'd been injured as a passenger in a car, I might have received hundreds of thousands of dollars in compensation. But us fellows who dive in the river more or less get kicked up the arse and told not to do it again. For me, it has been tough living on a pension of $315 a fortnight. Actually I am glad I never got compensated, because then I would never have worked in the Community Youth Support Service in Roma, and I don't think I would have written any poetry, let alone this book.

For I have taken up writing poems, and in a way I have shocked myself with the way some of them have turned out. I had never written a single poem until I broke my neck. I don't really call them 'poems' – they are my feelings, written down. When I was at school I hated the thought of writing poems or stories. No one ever taught me how to write poetry. After I broke my neck, I wouldn't talk or express what I was feeling in my heart. A few of the nurses told me to have a go at writing a poem. But that sounded so hard to me. To begin with, my negative attitude was that it was too hard. But when I moved to Roma, sometimes when I felt lonely or a bit depressed, I'd get a pen and a piece of paper and disappear to a nice quiet place outside. I soon found I was able to write out my feelings and that writing a poem wasn't as hard as I thought. My poetry was very personal and I didn't like to show it to anyone – I was afraid someone would say it was rubbish. I felt proud of my poems, but I was shy and lacked confidence. I have now written about sixty-five poems, and I'm still not sure whether they are good or bad. They are about my mates, horses, my dog, myself, my feelings and women.

Before I broke my neck I had plenty of girlfriends, but I can't honestly say that I've really been in love. I guess the nearest I came to it was with Michelle Bligh and another girl named Andrea. (The last time I heard of Andrea she was living with a bloke in Melbourne, so I give her my best and wish her well.) Girls like Michelle and Andrea come once in a million years.

Back when I was about ten years old, the more I saw of girls the more I liked horses. In some of my poems I express my feelings as I see the beauty of a horse, wild and untamed. I feel that the spirit of the brumby, like that of a human being, should remain free.

I have been seven years without a girlfriend. This was something I would never have thought possible. Without a girlfriend, the first two years were very hard and at times I felt lonely. Then I found I got used to being alone. While I was at Westhaven I had a few crushes on some of the girls in Roma. There was always someone sticking their nose in and giving me a lecture about how I would end up getting hurt. But if I went through seven years of not liking any girl at all then I wouldn't be human. I think, too, that everyone in a relationship, whether they're male or female, gets hurt at one stage of their lives. It makes no difference whether you are in a wheelchair or not. But I have come to realise that women aren't everything. I am pretty happy, overall, with the way things have turned out in the past seven years, and if the right girl does come along, who knows … I guess she would have to be pretty tough. If she doesn't come along, I guess you just have to say 'that's life'. And, as the saying goes, 'life's a bitch, but only if you let it be so'.

One thing I do watch is that I don't become too dependent on the people I am close to. Although I grew up with Peter and my sisters, I still find it hard to ask them to do anything for me. I was the same when I was in hospital at Brisbane and at Westhaven.

To be honest, I still reckon a dog is a man's best friend. You can talk to a dog and go down to the pub when you want to: your dog won't try to stop you. If I had a girlfriend who didn't want me to go to the pub, then all she would have to do is let the air out of my wheelchair tyres. That would leave me up shit creek without a paddle.

I've had a few frustrating experiences. Once I was sitting typing this manuscript when the splint fell off my finger and landed on the floor. Since I was the only one home I had to wait an hour and a half before someone came along to pick it up for me. Another time, at Westhaven, I felt like spitting out the dummy when I put a splint on to eat. No matter how hard I tried, I just couldn't get the right angle on my spoon to scoop up the food. One of the nurses came into my room and tightened up the splint and everything was okay. I am usually fairly patient, but when things which I normally find easy to do are not working then my patience turns to frustration.

Something that really pissed me off concerns my family. Two of my sisters had boyfriends who slapped them around. The thing that made it hard for me was that there was nothing I could do about it. Seven years ago I would have taken those blokes apart.

One time I started crying and swearing about being a quadraplegic in a wheelchair. It was the first time in seven years that I cracked up and let my temper get the best of me. I felt like packing up all my gear and going away, trying to forget what had happened and starting my life over again. Just worrying about myself. They say you shouldn't interfere in other people's fights. I reckon when it's your sister in the fight then you have the right to step in. Any brother who didn't do that would have to be a gutless wimp. Blokes like those have to realise that they don't own women. My favourite brother-in-law is Danny Halpin, who wouldn't raise a hand to anyone. He is a great bloke.

I can honestly say that I have never hit a woman. When I was fifteen, my mother told me that if ever I hit a woman she'd kill me. Recently I asked her, 'What would you do if I had a girl who punched me up?' Mum said: 'Nothing. You would probably have asked for it.'

Seven years in a wheelchair has been an experience. I look forward to the next seven years. I hope that maybe a few tetraplegics, quadraplegics and paraplegics will read this book. Maybe they'll realise it isn't so very difficult to write about your life. Everyone has different opinions and feelings and each story should make good reading. My advice to them is to have a go. I was frightened once and kept everything I wrote to myself. I never thought I could write a book by myself.

During the next seven years, if I drink a few less stubbies, chase a few more women and write another book, then I reckon you will be able to say that Billy Dodd's life is no longer full of 'ifs' or 'buts' as he comes face to face with reality.

11

This last chapter contains some of the poems I have written. As I said before, no one taught me how to write poetry. It was some of the nurses who first told me to have a go, to express what I was feeling inside my heart but found too difficult to talk about. When I moved to Roma, I sometimes used to get a bit lonely and depressed. So I would take a pen and paper and disappear to a nice quiet place outside. Soon I was writing down my feelings, and I discovered that writing a poem was not as hard as I had imagined. Although I felt proud of my poems, I lacked the confidence to show them to anyone. They were very personal, and I was afraid someone might say they were rubbish. I'm still not sure whether the poems are good or bad – I leave it to you to judge for yourself. And by the way – happy reading!

My Dad

This poem is dedicated to my Dad
Who passed away when I was a lad.
He left us crying, he left us sad –
He was the best we could have had.

We realised as time rolled by
In life there comes a time to die:
  A time to say goodbye,
  A time to ask: oh why
Why do these lovely people have to die?
  Some die young, some die old
  Some are the loved ones we used to hold.
  Is this how life is meant to be?

  Open your eyes, J.C.
  And please tell me
  In heaven what do you see –

Do you see a shy Aboriginal man
Riding those horses like only he can?
  That would be our old man.

J.D.

I owe a lot to this old fella
  He educated me in the bush
To me he stands above other men
  Yet he's only five foot four,
Not an inch less, not an inch more.

This old fella, my Dad's brother
  My Uncle John
He tried hard to keep me out of trouble.
He kicked me up the arse when I was wrong.
Now I look forward to seeing my Uncle J.D.
And I've thanked him for everything he did for me.

My uncle had a way with horses
When the devil inside them stirred.
He'd let out a '*cooee*', take off his hat
And sit a bucking horse like a magpie on heat.

J.D. put me on a big bay mare,
A mare that snorted, with fiery eyes
  A mare that was my downfall.
I landed in the dirt face-first
  But my uncle never said a word:
  He just grinned like a shot fox.

Next day I was back for another ride.
I caught the bay and stepped aboard.
The mare took off and began to buck –
  That bay mare, she threw me with ease
  Way up there in the nice cool breeze.

Shellie

Shellie looked at me with her big brown innocent eyes:
When my eyes met hers I fell in love.
I fell in love with a shy girl in denim jeans
I fell in love with a shy girl in a black T-shirt
I fell in love with a shy girl in pigtails
I fell in love with a girl named Shellie.

I held a hand so soft and gentle,
I kissed soft lips that spoke silent words.
When Shellie looked at me
She looked so innocent
She looked so young
And she looked so pretty.

We walked quietly hand in hand
With not a worry in the world.
Shellie put love in my heart,
Happiness in my life
And she taught me how to forgive.

I was only seventeen, in love with the prettiest girl
    I'd ever seen.
But we broke our promises
And in the end time tore us apart.
You screwed up my mind
And left a hole in my heart.

I wonder Shellie, are you sad like me
Or have you found the meaning of love,
With the giving of flowers
Or the joining of two hearts –
Two hearts to make one, man and wife.

You're in my dreams so far away
So far away I cannot reach.
But I see you in my dream
Standing alone, my teenage queen
I see you standing in the night,
But you disappear when I turn on the light.
Then I hear my mother knocking on my door.
She says: 'Go back to sleep, it's only half-past four.'

The Little Red Rose: Shannon

I've never been a priest
Learning how to help in a time of need
But I saw in her mother's eyes
The grief, the sadness
The heartbreak
That comes when a young child dies.

You find it hard,
Too young to understand
As questions go unanswered.
Her tender love untouched
Yesterday her rosy red cheeks
Brought happiness and love:
Today there is sadness and tears.

She gave us so much love
Before they took her away.
Only five months old
But so precious,
Spreading her love
With tender smiles
And cute brown eyes,
A child with angelic looks.

It's a sad day as grown men cry,
Tears fall gently to the ground
And disappear into the drought-stricken soil.

I wonder what her secrets were,
A little child so cute and cuddly,
So damn young and lovely.
She was our little Shannon Lesley.

That day we buried my little niece
And she took away a piece of my heart
With the love only a mother can give
She slipped away quietly in her sleep.

This poem is dedicated to my little niece, Shannon, who died from cot death syndrome. It broke our hearts; she was just five months old and she was so cute. This poem describes Shannon as a little red rose that bloomed for only five months.

The Little Red Rose: Sheldon

As I lay in bed
I heard the magpies chattering
The horses neighing
Babies crying
Nurses talking –

Talking about a new life.
For a baby boy had just been born.
A baby with beautiful big blue eyes.
He lay there like an angel in disguise,
Blossoming like a little red rose.

Still I lay in bed
As the magpies chattered
And the horses neighed,

While only one baby cried.
The nurse introduced me to my nephew,
And when I looked down at him
I knew a little red rose had been born.

He looked so young, he looked so small,
So innocent and fragile,
So much a little man.
Just like the opening of a rosebud
He brought us life,
He brought us beauty,
And he brought us happiness.
Sheldon, our little red rose.

After losing my niece, my nephew, Sheldon, was born. The two look so much alike: when I look at Sheldon, I can see a little red rose through his life and I know Shannon will never be forgotten, that innocent little child who promised us so much.

A Special Friend

He was just a playful pup,
A blue cattle dog with black spots.
To some people he was a mongrel,
  To others a rogue.
To me he was a true friend.

My pup looked like a dingo
Running in the wild.
He moved as silent as a fox stealing chickens.
People blamed him for things he didn't do –
But he did chase the postman for a lap or two.

He looked at me with innocent eyes
  Then ran closely by my side.
The day came when I left town
  And left my little pup all alone.
Where I was going he didn't know.
  Sadly, I never saw him again.

  Returning six years later
  I wanted to see my little blue pup,
But they told me my little mate had slipped away.
  I felt a tear run down my cheek:
The news hit me like an avalanche down a mountain.
  Another tear ran down my cheek

As I remembered the good times we used to have
The love I couldn't give
And the cows we never chased.

Reality

The silver stallion rears up on hind legs
He rears up to look over his hidden kingdom –
A kingdom hidden high in the hills.
As the sun sets in the silent shadows
He sights his mares running wild.

With fear in his heart
He sprints towards the group.
He sees a glare of fright in their eyes
And scents danger.
He sees a man with a gun in his hand.

As the silver stallion turns to protect his mares
He feels a stinging sensation.
He falls painfully to the ground,
The fight for freedom forgotten –
But he sees his mares running free.

He looks around at what once was his:
Through hazy eyes he looks at his kingdom
As his eyes close for the last time
He knows reality is greater than the dream.

After seven years with a broken neck I can still see the beauty in horses. Today, when I see a pretty horse from my wheelchair, deep down I am inspired to write a poem from my heart. In fact, since being in my wheelchair, my love for horses has grown. To write a poem about a horse was something I once thought would have been impossible.

Beauty Beyond My Dreams

The brown stallion is as pretty as a picture,
As wild and free as they come.
He runs as quick as the Texas wind
And disappears like a half-glimpsed spectre.

Identified by the star on his forehead
Or his four white feet,
He is chased by men with dreams –
Dreams that the brown stallion was theirs.

He looked his best when in full flight.
His mane whispered with the blowing of the wind.
He ran like a kite with a broken string.
His heart beat rapidly to every stride
As he ran away with a heart no one could touch.

Too beautiful to be called an outlaw,
Too fiery-eyed not to be one,
I was hypnotised by his beauty.
He possessed a beauty I had never seen before.
Yes, there stood the brown stallion,
The same stallion that had haunted me in my dreams.

I woke up shouting: 'Get my saddle!
He's here, the brown stallion!'
I awoke holding an empty lasso,
A lasso that had held one of the prettiest horses
  I'd ever seen.
Oh, what a pity it was all in a dream.

I like animals that are wild and free, especially the brumby. I reckon the brumbies should be left to run wild in the bush. But as the years pass, the brumby is becoming extinct. To me this is a real pity.

Phantoms of the Sun

Wild horses are haunting the night sky,
They're shining in the starlight.
Phantoms of the sun,
Once they roamed wild and free.
Their silent shadows now become
Victims to the drought.
Horses are shot and left to die,
Taken by man's ignorance.
Whole-hearted horses haunting the plain,
Beauty running with the wind:
Let them go, let them be free,
Let them shine in the starlight,
These phantoms of the sun.

Running Free

A pretty little Palomino pony ran wildly through the gate.
I could sense her fear but not the hate.
The men had never seen an outlaw horse come any meaner –
This was the wild filly they called Tina.

Trapped, Tina stood trembling in the yard.
Her nostrils breathed fire,
Her eyes showed fear.
Silently she stood awaiting a showdown.

I threw a lasso that landed over her proud head.
Tina unleashed, with the venom and movement of a deadly snake.
I witnessed an unseen evil,
An evil possessed by the devil.

Her movements were short and swift.
Her silky mane sparkled in the yellow sun:
As she turned her beauty shone.

She carried her neck with an arch like a rainbow,
Her beauty matched only by the grace of a black swan.
I placed my saddle upon her back:
Nervously she watched my every move.

I climbed aboard and all was right:
I felt like a king upon his throne.
Suddenly she felt the spurs bite –
And that's when I found that kings are made to be dethroned.
Tina's untamed spirit could not be broken
Her heart could not be tamed
The bush is where she belonged.
Running wild
Running free
Running for us all to see.

The Cold South Wind Blowing

The old stockmen sitting around the campfire
Felt the cold chill of a south wind blowing.
The south wind is as cold as cold can be:
  So they snuggle up into their swags,
  Trying to hide from that south wind.

  The men look up at the stars,
The stars shining in the lonely night.
Up in the sky they see the most wonderful light
As three beautiful horses appear from nowhere,
  Just as though they were angels,
Angels being blown around by the south wind.

No one spoke, they just sat and stared:
As the horses came nearer the stockmen froze,
  Paralysed by such beauty,
  Beauty seen only in dreams.
  The more they looked
The more they were possessed.
The men could see the sparkle in the horses' eyes.

The horses sped across the night sky
Moving with speed, elegance and grace,
And a moment later
They were carried away by the south wind.

This poem is based on a dream I had one night. When you read it, I hope you can picture three beautiful horses gliding across the sky.

Thoughts in My Head

I'm lying here in bed:
Paralysed body, nerves are dead.
The sun reflects off the shiny glass.
After a cold night there's dew on the grass.
I'm lying here with thoughts in my head.

I never slept too well last night:
I dreamt of '83, when things were right.
I dreamt of the legs I once took for granted,
Girls, and the horses I've cantered.
I'm lying here with thoughts in my head.

Paralysed from the chest down, a body without feeling,
Thoughts in my head, my eyes turned to the ceiling.
Maybe I might watch something on television,
Flick through the channels to the ABC …

But they say 'where there's a will there's a way'.
  As I watch the passing of another day
  I'm lying here with thoughts in my head.

Give Me a Go

I feel down in spirit,
Disheartened and defeated …
Don't know which way to turn
Don't know where to go.

For me the sun is not shining:
The sky is turning black.
I'm surrounded by shitty people.
My smile has turned to a smirk.
I feel it is time to say goodbye.

To find a place where the skies are blue,
A place where the sun is shining,
The horses are playing,
People are smiling.

I take life in its stride –
Sometimes that's not enough.
I ask for help, but I fall prey,
A victim to shitty people.

I find it hard relying on others.
I have no choice.
Why don't they understand
My skies are turning black,

My smile is a smirk.
Wake up, you shitty people.
All I ask is – give me a go.

Gone Wrong

I sit here thinking,
Thinking about a young man gone wrong.
Wild and woolly in his ways,
He was a kid growing up before his time.
He never said 'no' to a fight,
He never learnt from his mistakes.
His heart was wild and so were his ways,
This kid growing up before his time.

His horse, Four X, could do no wrong –
Nor could his mate, a bloke named Chong.
Downtown they'd go for a ride,
Four X and Chong, side by side.
Sixteen years of age and so headstrong –
He was wild and rather young.
He fought a battle with the police,
Took them on in the street,
This kid growing up before his time.

Now I sit here thinking
Inside a body gone dead.
My horse is made of steel
My legs have lost their feeling.
My mind is at rest.
I no longer say 'yes' to a fight.

I've been shot through the heart –
But for me life goes on, no matter what.
So I'll make do with what I've got.

Just Billy

To some he was a bad bugger
To others a teenage rebel.
  He ran wild and free
Untamed as only a wild one can be.

He took life in his stride,
Chasing women, breaking horses to ride.
  He found out right from wrong
Created a life of fun and leisure:
A teenage rebel, or so they said.

Five years later I saw him in a wheelchair.
He gave me a look of frustration
  A look of despair.

  Brown eyes disheartened
  Brown eyes dispirited
  Brown eyes dejected
  Brown eyes defeated.
Brown eyes, spirited, wild and free
Brown eyes broken momentarily.
    Billy Dodd ponders
  On what might have been.
He thinks of the horses he never rode
  The places he has never seen
The babies he may never have
The missed opportunities in life.

A spirit like his is hard to break
For this heart is not ready to take.
But, Billy, you bounced back like an egg dropped on cement.
You picked up the pieces
You lived with a broken neck
You're no longer a teenage rebel
But in the town of Mitchell
You still run wild and free
Still untamed as only Billy Dodd can be.

Today when I go downtown in my wheelchair and talk to different people, some tell me I used to be a wild bugger, while others say I was a rogue. So I wrote this poem and dedicated it to myself. Hopefully, some who read it may understand what I felt at times. To tell the truth, a lot of people in Mitchell have been good to me and made life in a wheelchair so much easier, which I appreciate deeply.

Acknowledgements

Besides the doctors, hospital staff and mates I talk about in my book, I would like to mention the following very special people, who have all helped me in so many ways.

At the Princess Alexandra Hospital Spinal Unit: Andrea, Michele Cahill, 'Crimmie', Helena, and Jenny Kennedy.

At Westhaven and in Roma: Kerry Batley, Kay Burnes, Debbie Carmichael, Lee-Ette Clifford, Bev Coburn, Marie Connell, Judy Connolly, Paula Giles, Debbie Ison, Lesley McEwan, Julie, Kaylene and Sharon Newbolt and their parents Johnny and Marie, Cliff Orchard, Adriana Pellari, Allan Platz, Sue Primus, Mary Ramage, Marina Smith, Lyn Sullivan, Kylie Swan.

In Mitchell, my home town: Colin and Normie Finlay and their parents Bobby and Joyce, and Stevo Foster.

To all these people: thanks!

Bill Dodd